To: Lady Helen
I bless You in th[illegible]ne
of Yeshu.

Shalom
Fidel M. Donaldson
09-27-15

DON'T BIRTH AN ISHMAEL IN THE WAITING ROOM

"All the days of my appointed time will I wait, till my change come."
— Job 14:14b

Fidel M. Donaldson

ISBN: 978-0-578-00639-0

Unless otherwise stated, quotations from the Bible are from the King James Version.

LCCN: 2009900393

Printed in the United States of America

TABLE OF CONTENTS

This book is dedicated to King Jesus. My Savior and Lord

Much Love To:

My wife for life, Paulette Donaldson, and all our Children
The SWAT Team (Soldiers Watching and Travailing)
Special thanks to Dr. Inskip Allsop for editing the manuscript
My father in the Lord: Dr. Samuel N. Greene

Minister José R. Vargas: Elder Martin Montantine: Minister Rhodora James: Prophetess Tasha Edwards

FOREWORD

There comes a time in every Christian's life when a change occurs. Something happens where what is, can no longer be, and what will be, starts coming closer and closer to fruition. However, it is in that span of time, that space, between what is and what will be, where the dedicated decide and the unsure become unraveled.

Ask any expectant parent what the most trying part of the birthing process is and they will tell you it is the wait. The pain of delivery is nothing compared to the wear and tear, impatience, and anxiety of the wait. So, too, when birthing in the spiritual realm, learning to wait is *of utmost importance*. In fact, waiting is so significant; Satan has set himself and his minions against it. Their battle cry is "Now! Want it now! Get it now! Have it now! Do it now! Now! Now! Now!"

Waiting is what the waiting room was created for. You may sleep, you may eat, you may talk, you may even read in the waiting room, but the reality is that all of those activities are simply done to pass the time **as you wait.** *Don't Birth an Ishmael in the Waiting Room* teaches you how to do just that: wait in God's waiting room of delay. And wait in such a way that you will see the true purpose of waiting: preparation, purification, and promotion.

As you read this book, take the time to digest each word so it becomes real to you. By so doing, you will become intimate with the Truth of God, and be impregnated by the Spirit that is within that Truth. You will feel the purpose gestate in you, and finally, you will experience the birth pangs...and you will push...and push…and give birth to the promise. Then, as you hold that beautiful "baby", you will know that the birth of this promise was because you held on and waited, unlike Abraham and Sarah who grew weary and anxious and gave birth to an Ishmael. You will know this and you will rejoice.

May God bless you beyond belief as you peruse these pages.

I congratulate you in advance on the birth of your new "baby". Hallelujah!!!

Minister José R. Vargas

AUTHOR'S NOTE

There are many people in life waiting for many things. Some are waiting for husbands while others wait for wives. Some wait to matriculate while some wait to graduate. Each person will invariably deal with a certain level of anxiety that is correlated and proportional to the level of importance of the thing for which they are waiting. The challenge for all of us is to avoid acting impatiently or impulsively for that will ultimately cause us more difficulty than the waiting itself.

In this book, I compare the experience of the child of God who is waiting for the fulfillment of a promise to that of a woman during pregnancy and the birthing process; from the anticipation of pregnancy, to conception to delivery. I intend to examine the waiting experience by drawing heavily on this parallel which bears so many analogous elements; it may surprise you how similar they are. I will give the reader Biblical examples of individuals who messed up while waiting and of individuals who exercised patience while waiting. In this treatise, Ishmael symbolizes that which the child of God births in the flesh while waiting to birth the promise of God.

First off, let me take this opportunity to apologize to every woman that has ever given birth for presuming to speak on the subject. Not only do I lack expertise on the subject of conceiving, carrying, and delivering a baby, but I doubt that any a man can really comprehend what it takes to go through that process, because, as the Jamaican saying goes, only he—in this case, she—who feels it knows it. There is one thing a woman can do that a man can never even dream of accomplishing: conceiving, carrying and then giving birth to a new life. Women seem to have been given some hidden reservoir of strength to do this and the many other tasks of child-rearing and nurturing. Men, on the other hand, are prone to faint in the delivery room just watching, to speak nothing of the reticence with which they usually get involved in the care of the new baby. (This is probably the reason why from the time of Jesus until now, the lion's share of the work of ministry has been done by women.) That said, however, I do believe that both men and women can draw lessons from the birthing process that can be applied to the spiritual "promise-birthing" process. If understood, and appropriately applied, these lessons/parallels can provide a very useful template that will aid every believer in conceiving, carrying, and birthing the prophetic word or vision with which the Spirit of God has impregnated them.

It is not God's desire for any born again, Spirit-filled believer to suffer spiritual barrenness. The Lord expects each of us to birth something great. That is why He has invested so richly in us. We will have to endure the hardships and challenges of gestation and labor like any expectant mother, but if we are willing to do so, we can count on our spiritual midwife, the Holy Spirit, to help us bring forth our "baby".

A woman carrying a child in her womb will go through various bodily changes during the first, second, and third trimesters, and a believer waiting to birth the Lord's vision for his or her life will similarly go through various changes during each stage of the process. I trust this book will be insightful and encouraging as we all labor to birth that holy thing that the Lord has placed in us.

CHAPTER 1
SEPARATION FOR PREPARATION

> *"But when it pleased God, who separated me from my mother's womb, and called me by his grace, To reveal his Son in me, that I might preach him among the heathen; immediately I conferred not with flesh and blood" (Galatians 1: 15-16).*

What is the place of your separation? Is it a prison cell? Is it a body that is infirmed with sickness that causes constant pain? Or is it having to move to a new place, away from all that is familiar and loved? Have you allowed circumstances to embitter you and cripple your confession of faith? Can you rise above that place and give God the glory? Like the little maid in second Kings Chapter 5, can you speak words of edification that will bring someone else deliverance in spite of your captivity? Esther was separated from her homeland and taken captive to Persia but the Sovereign God allowed her to find favor and become Queen. She had no idea she would go from being a slave to a Queen and God would use her to save her people. Joseph was a slave in Egypt but the Sovereign God allowed him to be second in charge and to have a positive impact on his family, the Egyptians, and the surrounding nations.

Before preparation can take place for the birthing of purpose; before any time spent in the waiting room of preparation, there must be separation. God must first separate our spirit from all that would hold us captive—be that the easily besetting sin, or the familiar and comfortable—so that He may lead us to where we can fully embrace the promise and He can effectually promote and use us. He does this because people, places and things can hinder the process, and He will not allow anyone, anything or any place to hinder His plans for our life. So don't despise the place where you are today. Find a way to bring the presence of the Lord into that place. God is in charge of your life and He can get glory out of any situation.

My Testimony: Separated From My Easily Besetting Sin

I remember a time in my life when I was headed down a path of death and destruction because I had refused to heed the advice of the people who loved me. I was totally consumed by carnal pleasures. I dealt drugs, partied, fornicated and committed adultery with reckless abandon. My wife tried to witness to me but my response was, "Get out of here with that white man's religion. Fools go to church on Sunday." My soul was consumed by bitterness and hatred because of some of the injustices I had suffered growing up in the city of New York. There is never an excuse for sin, because the blood of Jesus is the antidote for sin but I felt I my early hardships gave me license to be reckless. Success in carnal things can give a person an air of invincibility and God has to do some stripping to get the person's attention. I was the type of person that had to be stripped of carnality to be clothed with righteousness.

Cockiness and arrogance dulled my senses and caused me to become impervious to the slippery slope I was sliding down. God would have to do something drastic to separate me from the filthy lifestyle that was engrossing and slowly suffocating me. Intercessory prayer was the instrument used by God to separate me from the shackles. When intercessors get you in their crosshairs it is only a matter of time before the Lord apprehends you. There were times I came home in a drunken stupor and saw my wife and some prayer warriors in our apartment praying. She never badgered or threatened me; she just took me to the Lord in prayer and patiently waited for my deliverance. I remember staggering by them and heading to my bedroom, oblivious to the fact that they had me on the altar and that it was only a matter of time before the God of Heaven arrested me. During that same period, my sister and a friend were also praying for me on a weekly basis. Jesus said there is a kind that only comes out through prayer and fasting. Well, I was that kind. *Tide* couldn't take my sin away nor could *Oxy-clean* get the stain out. Calgon couldn't take my sin away and Shout could not get it out. Only the Blood of Jesus could do that. My wife knew that God had a plan for my life and I would need a wake up call for that plan to unfold.

The wakeup call came in November of 1990 when I was arrested in England for conspiracy to smuggle drugs into that country. God was about to birth a new creature out of the waste places of my life and the birthing room would be a prison cell. Jesus was laid in a manger when He was born and I believe the Father allowed that to happen so no one could use a lowly birth place as an excuse for a lack of achievement. The son of God was birthed in a stable with animals so you must understand that it is not how you came into this world that matters but what you do while you are here to better yourself and humanity.

Something that appears to be tragic can be the very thing God uses to save lives. I am firmly convinced that the Lord allowed me to go to prison to save my life and give me eternal life. I was taken to one of London's notorious jails called Worm Wood Scrubs, and placed on 23 hour a day lockdown in a small cell that had no toilet. Believe me when I tell you, you will "wake up quickly and smell the coffee" when your freedom is taken away from you. God separated the sinner man from his street friends, his wife, his children and all that was familiar so He could deal with the inner man. I had refused to heed the call when I was free in New York so He allowed me to be captured and imprisoned in England so I would wake up and recognize the seriousness of my transgressions. It is very sad to note that there are many men and women who refuse to surrender to Jesus even after repeated warnings, and repeated imprisonments until they are given long sentences in prison. And there are some who still refuse to get the message even behind bars.

I spent a year on remand at Worm Wood Scrubs, Brixton, and another facility called Swaleside, when I received an 8 year sentence without parole. That meant that, with good behavior, I would be out in 5 years and 3 months, which probably would not happen because it is difficult to have good behavior when you are surrounded by other criminals. Time in a prison cell, separated from familiar people, places and things, will force you to do a great deal of self analysis and introspection. For the first time in my life I had to come to terms with the decisions I had made that had led me to that point in my life. I had to take off the rose-colored glasses of self-deception and begin to look at myself as I really was. There were no women at my beck and call, nor champagne in the night clubs, nor expensive costumes, nor sweet smelling perfumes, nor expensive jewelry. There I was in my prison-issued clothes, locked down with other criminals who, like me, had become a number. The cockiness and the arrogance had given way to a sense of regret and melancholy as I tried to come to terms with the fact that I was about to be put away for many years. I had been arrested years before in New York but I was able to beat the case in a jury trial. I had learned nothing from that first experience. Actually, I was embolden by the fact that I had won the case and had gone out celebrating with some of the *rude boys* I hung around, right after the victory.

God Bless The Gideon Society

You have to find creative ways to keep yourself from dying of boredom and worry when you are locked in a small cell for 23 hours a day, waiting to be tried by a jury and potentially facing a lengthy jail sentence. I did a lot of pushups and read all the magazines and newspapers I got my hands on. One day I found a small *New Testament and Psalms* in the dresser drawer and began to read it. It had been placed in the prison by the Gideon Bible Society. I had categorically rejected Christianity because my mind was obscured by racism and could not get past the picture of the longhaired white man people had hanging in their homes and some churches. I had no concept of the power of the real Jesus, but He was about to reveal Himself to me.

The watershed moment came for me on March 6, 1991, when I was reading John Chapter 5. No preacher was in the cell giving an impassioned plea for sinners to come and be washed in the fount that flows from Emmanuel's veins, as the choir sets the atmosphere with songs like "What Can Wash Away My Sins." But as I read of the Pharisees' attack on Jesus for healing the man that sat at the pool of Bethesda, the Holy Spirit began to chip away at the fallow ground of my stony heart. I didn't know it at the time, but Bethesda means House of Mercy. The pool had five porches, and five is the number for grace. The Sovereign God of the universe was drawing me to Himself through grace and mercy. I heard the voice of the real Jesus calling me that day, and after a great struggle with the carnal mind, I knelt down and surrendered to Him. I was still physically a prisoner, but my mind and soul were freed that day.

My life was transformed immediately and I went about testifying to great and small about His goodness. In His wisdom He allowed me to receive His salvation before I was sentenced to 8 years. I didn't know it at the time but 8 is the number of new beginnings. God's grace and mercy are the vehicles that make salvation possible because without them we would be consumed by His wrath. The salvation He provided me not only gave me eternal life, but it gave me peace to deal with the contrary voices that whispered in my ear that I would never see freedom again. I had to fight against the spirit of fear and doubt that tried to take hold of me when I found out that there was an attempt to indict me in a conspiracy case in the Midwest. God gave me victory in that case and, in just three short years; three is the number which represents resurrection. I was able to walk free from my incarceration in England because He planned to use me to win the lost at any cost. My incarceration seemed like a negative at first but I thank God for it because it is from that experience that I came to know Jesus as Lord and Savior. If I had had my choice, I would have chosen to receive salvation in a beautiful sanctuary after a great message, with all my family around. But there was no way I would have listened prior to my incarceration because my mind was too debauched and steeped in sin. God's ways are not ours and we must trust Him because He knows our ending from our beginning. There are times when He causes us to be separated from a familiar, comfortable place and taken to a hard place. But we must not lose hope for God's purpose in doing so is to cleanse our temple from the things that defile us. In order to use me and place His seed within me, God had to separate me from my former lifestyle and place me in the waiting room of a jail cell, away from all the comforts of life and the things that made God an unnecessary and undesired commodity. That separation became my divorce from Sin and my marriage to Christ.

The Prodigal Son, Separated By Rebellion and Ingratitude

One of the stories which captivated my attention during my incarceration was The Prodigal Son. Jesus used this story to counteract the criticisms of the Pharisees when they murmured against him for eating with, and receiving sinners. In the story, the Father represents God, the older son, the Pharisees, and the younger son, sinners separated from the Father's house. The Bible says, "*And the younger of them said to his father, Father, give me the portion of goods that falleth to me. And he divided unto them his living. And not many days after the younger son gathered all together, and took his journey into a far country, and there wasted his substance with riotous living*" (Luke 15:12-13).

He broke the order of inheritance and the laws of primogeniture by requesting that his father give him his portion of the inheritance. His request was disrespectful because he was the younger of two sons and his father was still alive. In the International Standard Bible Encyclopedia on page 1, James Orr defines primogeniture as, "*The right of the firstborn to inherit the headship of the family, carrying with it certain property rights and usually such titles as those of the high-priesthood or kingship*". In giving Biblical examples, Orr writes, "*In the most ancient genealogies, a distinction is drawn between the firstborn and the other son (Gen 10:15; 22:21; 25:13; 35:23; 36:15). In the bestowal of parental blessings in patriarchal times great importance was attached to preferring the firstborn (Gen 25:31; 27:29; 48:13; 49:3). The feud between Jacob and Esau (Gen 27:1 through 28:21) grew out of the stealing of the firstborn's blessing by the younger brother. Joseph was displeased when, in his blessing, Jacob seemed to prefer Ephraim to Manasseh, his firstborn (Gen 48:18). The father in such cases seems to have had the right to transfer the birthright from one son to another, from the days of Abraham in the case of Ishmael and Isaac, through those of Jacob in the matter of Reuben and Joseph and in the matter of Ephraim and Manasseh, down to the days of David in the selection of a successor to the kingship.*" The father could choose to bestow on the younger son the blessing of the firstborn, but **it was not the younger son's place** to make a request for his inheritance.

Once his father acquiesced, the son separated himself from the protection and security of his father's house and traveled to a far country so he could revel in carnality. The significance of his traveling to a far country is that it gives us a picture of how far the rebellious sinner is willing to travel to get away from the order and structure of the Father's house. The fact that he gathered all together shows his intention to sever all ties. Sin will take you farther than you want to go, keep you longer than you want to stay, and cost you more than you want to pay. There are many people languishing behind prison walls now, wishing they had listened to a father, a mother, or someone who tried to warn them about the consequences of their destructive lifestyle.

Once the younger son's finances ran out he began to suffer because there was a mighty famine in the land. He was forced to join himself to a citizen of that country who sent him into his fields to feed the swine. Familiarity breeds contempt and people often develop a contemptuous attitude towards things that are readily available to them. How true that was of the younger son. He had separated himself from his father's house because he had lost appreciation for the blessings that being in his father's house provided. It took a stay in the pigpen to open up his eyes and bring him to his senses. Sometimes God has to separate some of us from the pleasant and comfortable and put us into difficult places where our flesh can be humbled and crucified. Pride, rebellion and stubbornness are killing many people and the bed of affliction is the only way God can get their attention. He has no problem afflicting the body in order to save the soul.

The son that was once blessed and privileged to be in his father's house found himself desiring the husks the pigs ate because no one gave him anything to eat. The Bible doesn't say that he was trying to eat the *corn,* but that he was trying to get to the husks. There was no corn there! In scripture corn is a symbol of harvest, increase and blessing. This shows us how desperate his situation had become. The verses describing his desire to eat the husks the pigs ate became real to me when I found out that the bags of oatmeal I ate in the English prison had a stamp on them that read *pig's meal*. The prison I was sent to serve my sentence was called Swaleside and it was located near a pig farm. When the wind blew, the stench of the sty would invade my cell and suffocate me. The pigpen will humble you and force you to recognize that you are not the center of the universe and the world does not revolve around you.

It is no surprise that most born again believers had a pivotal point in their life when they faced a situation where they had to look to their Heavenly Father for survival. Most people don't turn to God when things are going well; it is usually a crisis situation that drives them to the cross, and this son was no different. His life typifies that of every sinner who, because of sin, lives separated from Abba, Father. His life also exemplifies what a person must do when their sinful action plunges them into the pigpen of hardship. The Bible says, *"And when he came to himself, he said, How many hired servants of my father's have bread enough and to spare, and I perish with hunger!"* (Luke 15:17).

His circumstance did not change until he came to himself. He had to come to the realization that his own actions had led him to the pigsty. Many individuals are having difficulty learning the lesson God is trying to teach them in the pigsty. They refuse to come to themselves and make an honest assessment of the sty they are living in and the vomit in which they continue to wallow. How many hits of crack, how many snorts of cocaine and heroin, and how many prison sentences do you need to serve; how long must you be separated from your child or children to realize that crime does not pay, it costs? It costs the family of the inmates the pain of separation. It costs the wife; it costs the children time separated from their father or mother; time they will never be able to redeem. How long will you have to suffer before you come to yourself and realize that sin is dragging you to a dark place? A place of no return unless you grab the lifeline Jesus has extended to you.

Come to yourself and cry out to your Heavenly Father in repentance. After coming to himself, the prodigal son said, *"How many hired servants of my father's have bread enough and to spare, and I perish with hunger! I will arise and go to my father, and will say unto him, Father, I have sinned against heaven, and before thee, And am no more worthy to be called thy son: make me as one of thy hired servants"* (Luke 15: 17-19). By giving him a glimpse of the true nature of his rebellion and desires, God was able to begin the process of separation that would lead this young man back home and to his fore-ordained purpose.

In the same manner Nebuchadnezzar came to himself after finally looking up: "*And at the end of the days I Nebuchadnezzar lifted up mine eyes unto heaven, and mine understanding returned unto me, and I blessed the most High, and I praised and honored him that liveth for ever, whose dominion is an everlasting dominion, and his kingdom is from generation to generation"* (Dan 4:34). You, too, must make the decision to lift up your eyes to Heaven and the Most High will cause you to rise out of the pit you presently find yourself in.

Remember, the journey of a thousand miles begins with the first step, and the first step to reconciliation is repentance. Once you recognize the wretchedness of the pigsty, you must arise. Arise from lust and perversion; arise from drug addiction; arise from un-forgiveness and the spirit of pride that keep you in the pigsty unwilling to forgive. Arise with a spirit of humility and recognize that nothing will change as long as you refuse to learn what the Father is trying to teach you. The prodigal rose from the stench of the sty and headed to his father's house in repentance. He confessed *to his father* that he was a sinner, unworthy to be called a son. Instead, he would accept just being one of the hired servants. After all, the servants had bread enough to spare. While the servants were walking in increase and overflow, he the son was living in poverty. There are many sons and daughters who are away from the Father's house living in squalor, and all they need to do is repent. Repent means more than saying, "I'm sorry." Repent means to turn from where you are and head back to the Father. It means to take the step of separation from your evil past to your righteous future as a son or daughter of God.

Take note that when he went to his father for the portion of his inheritance he had said, "Father, give me." However, after spending time in the pigsty, competing with the hogs for the husks, he now pleads, "Make me." This is the purpose of the separation: to get us to the place where we will desire the Father to "make us" instead of looking to Him to "give us". Like the woman who must "leave" or "separate" from father and mother to "become" a man's wife, God can only "make us" if we allow Him to "separate us" from our former life and attitudes, and that separation begins in the mind and spirit of a person when they recognize that being one with God is far superior to the life of sin they once cherished. His father saw him from a great distance and had compassion on him. Don't believe the devil's lie when he tries to convince you that the country sin has carried you to is so distant that you are out of your Heavenly Father' sight. He not only sees you, but He waits for you to return so that He may restore and celebrate you. The father told the servants to bring the best robe for His returning son so that the tattered rags of his rebellion and shame might be covered. This robe signified to all that the son was not only being restored, but that he was now standing in an improved position than before. The father also commanded that a ring be put on his son's right hand. The ring symbolized eternity, authority and power in another's name, while right hand was symbolic of blessings and righteousness. The shoes that were put on his feet represented his restored walk with the Father. And for every prodigal son or daughter that has left the Father's house and traveled to the far country, God wants you to know that when the famine comes—and it will come—if you will come to yourself and turn back to Him, He will restore you. Second Chronicles 7:14 says, *"if my people which are called by my name, shall humble themselves, and pray, and seek my face, and turn from their wicked ways; then will I hear from heaven, and will forgive their sin, and will heal their land."*

When the Father killed the fatted calf (which symbolizes partaking of that which has been prepared beforehand for us) and held a celebration for the younger son, his elder brother became jealous and refused to come into the house. He reminded his father of what the younger brother had done with the inheritance, how he had devoured his living with harlots. The self-righteous Pharisees, of whom the elder brother is a type, will always attempt to point out our sins before the Father. But when we repented and returned to Him, He chose to forget them, so it really doesn't matter who chooses to remember them. He has thrown them into the sea of forgetfulness, to be remembered no more. Don't worry about the religious people who go fishing in the cesspool of your past. They are jealous because they see God showering you with His grace and mercy. What they fail to grasp is that you humbled yourself and allowed Him to cleanse you through the pain of separation. God separated you from your past to birth in you a glorious future of liberty. So walk in the authority and restoration that God has provided for you, and do not allow anyone to entangle you with the yoke of bondage.

Paul, Separated On The Road To Damascus

"And what agreement hath the temple of God with idols? for ye are the temple of the living God; as God hath said, I will dwell in them, and walk in them; and I will be their God, and they shall be my people. Wherefore come out from among them, and be ye separate, saith the Lord, and touch not the unclean thing; and I will receive you" (2 Corinthians 6:16-17). A great miracle takes place when the Lord delivers an individual from the bondage of sin and prepares him to do a great work. When we look at some of

the people He chose to use, we realize that He is a God that is merciful and full of grace. Many of us would not have chosen some of the people He chose.

Paul uses the same Greek word for *separate* in 2 Corinthians 6 that he used when he told the Galatians that God had separated him from his mother's womb. In other words, God has *set us apart* from the distracting influences of our lives. We have to be separated and prepared to enter into the Most Holy Place to commune with God. The Lord will not receive us if we have idols in our lives, or contaminate ourselves by touching the unclean. Though we are in the world, we must not be of the world. In other words, we must not allow the world's system to pollute our minds. Before the Lord receives a person or thing, it must be consecrated, purified and dedicated to him for His use. As such, we must examine our lives daily to determine if there is anything that has become an idol. Likewise, we must scrutinize our relationships, recognizing that one of the devil's main entry points into our lives is people. Association brings assimilation, so we must learn to discern the spirit behind the people we associate with in order to determine if these relationships are producing spiritual fruit. You can tell a great deal about a person by looking at the people he associates with. That means that our friendships are impacting our spiritual lives whether we are conscious of that fact or not. My grandmother always told me, "show me your company and I will tell you who you are." You know the old saying, "Birds of a feather flock together." Have you ever seen an eagle hanging with buzzards or chickens? So stop hanging around with buzzards. Stop acting like a chicken and allow God to unfold his plan for your life, so you can soar like the eagle you are. It is for that reason the Bible commands us to "... come out from them and be **separate** ...Touch no unclean thing, and I will receive you." (2 Corinthians 6:17).

God redeemed us with the precious, priceless blood of His only son, Jesus, thus indicating the value He has placed in us and the greatness of His plan for us. That is what the apostle Paul told the Ephesians: *"That in the ages to come he might shew the exceeding riches of his grace in his kindness toward us through Christ Jesus"* (Ephesians 2:7). Now it is up to us to allow Him to separate us from everything that might interfere with His plan for our lives. This separation might be painful and may call for sacrifices, but we cannot afford to let our natural inclination to avoid change and its accompanying discomfort, prevent us from moving forward with God. Let the contemplation of Jesus' ultimate sacrifice for us deliver us from our stagnation and prepare us for our separation.

Paul didn't use any excuses to avoid his "separation" when God called him. He didn't tell the Lord He could not preach in His name because he had persecuted Christians and been there when Stephen was stoned. He didn't think about what his former colleagues in the Sanhedrin would think or what it would cost him to accept the call. He simply surrendered to the plan of God and allowed Him to be glorified in and through his life. In spite of the great authority he had as a Pharisee—especially as a member of the Sanhedrin- he was willing to be separated from that lifestyle for the Glory of God. One can only imagine how much the Pharisees hated him because of his dedication to the call of God to preach Jesus. We must be delivered from people's opinions if we are to fulfill our assignment. We must do what God has called us to do even if it means we will lose some friends and family.

Just as the Apostle Paul didn't vacillate or seek the approval of men, but asked, *"Lord, what wilt thou have me to do?"* (Acts 9:6), so, too, should every Christian respond when called by the Lord for a Kingdom assignment. Far too many believers, on receiving God's call to separate from certain people, places, and things so that they might be better prepared to carry out their commission, refuse to move because they are bound by the opinions of men. They allow flesh and blood to determine their course of action. While God can, and may speak through flesh and blood, and we should respect the opinions of Godly people, ultimately, we must be obedient to the call of God on our lives as it is revealed to our conscience and spirit.

Others allow their fears and misgivings to keep them back. We see this brought out in the call of Moses, Jeremiah and Gideon. When the Lord called Moses, he tried to hide behind his speech impediment. Similarly, Jeremiah expressed concerns about his age. Gideon told the Lord that his family was poor and that he was the least in his father's house. These three great men of God proffered excuses to avoid following where God wanted to lead them. But God simply squelched those excuses by reasserting the call. Excuses will keep a person average and prevent him or her from walking in the fullness of God's purpose for his or her life. Many men and women of God today have missed crucial seasons in their life because they did not move when God called, offering up instead, excuses. If you know there is a call of God on your life, stop procrastinating and making excuses. Yield to His will so He can use you to His honor and glory. And remember: When we stand before Him on judgment day and are judged based on how we invested the talents He gave us (see Luke 19:12—22), we will have no excuses, for He will accept none.

The natural mind cannot fathom God's ways because His ways are not our ways. The incomprehensible, sometimes, perplexing operations of God, often leave us wondering if God knows what He is doing. For instance, why would God "separate" and call a man who wreaked havoc on the early church and gave his full energy towards annihilating it? Because He is Omniscient and He knew exactly the course that Paul would take. He knew that, in his Pharisaical ignorance, Paul would zealously persecute the church for spreading the Good News about His Son. But He also knew that, once his eyes were opened, He would find in Paul someone so grateful for the grace he received, he would willingly endure shipwrecks, beatings, stoning and the constant threat of death just to let the whole world know about the love of God.

(Perhaps there never has been another individual who understood, appreciated, and did as much to spread the word about the Lord's grace and mercy like the Apostle Paul.) No one knew then—and certainly not Paul—that God would use him to write two thirds of the New Testament, take the Gospel to all of the then-known world and establish so many congregations. But God knew. God knew that in spite of his shaky beginning, He could still use Paul mightily.

God also knew that the work Paul had to do could not be done by just anyone. He needed a devout, incisive and decisive man who was well versed in the law to counteract those that would try to draw people back from grace into legalism. Apostle Andre Cook said, *"It is out of our mess that God gives us a message for this messed up age."* God can use anyone to speak to a prostitute, a drug addict, or someone caught up in sexual perversion, but when someone from the aforementioned group is used by God, they witness from a personal perspective because God delivered them from the same pit. Their witness carries a certain amount of weight because they can empathize with the person that is going through what they went through. It is one thing when a person tells you that God *can* deliver, but it is much more effective when they tell you that he *has* delivered.

There are many things that are alien to us in terms of Gods preparation of our divine assignment, but we can rest assured that God knows our ending from our beginning and He has brought us out of sin to bring us into His kingdom. God separates us for His purpose, defined as, "the reason for which a person or thing is created." We were created to bring glory to God but sin caused us to miss the mark. Therefore God has to separate us to prepare us to birth His purpose.

Paul's was a radical conversion in the sense that he was a Pharisee and Pharisees considered heathens to be unclean. They hated Jesus because He took time to eat and fellowship with people they considered ritually unclean. When God commissioned

Paul on the Damascus Road he was blinded by the light that shone from heaven and was three days without sight. God was giving him a new vision and was about to show him things he'd never seen before. The Lord spoke to a man named Ananias and sent him to speak to Paul. Ananias was reluctant because he had heard the report of how much evil Paul had done to the saints at Jerusalem. God told Ananias that Paul was a chosen vessel, and He would show Paul how many things he would have to suffer for His name.

When the Lord chooses a vessel to set it apart for His purpose, a major part of the preparation process is the furnace of affliction. Chosen vessels will be tested and will suffer for the Name of the Lord. This is not a welcomed truth but it is truth nonetheless. As a Pharisee Paul was tenacious and relentless in his persecution of Christians so the Lord knew how much greater his tenacity would be once he received a true revelation of who Christ was. That revelation gave him the strength and the courage to endure all the affliction and persecution that he endured when he began to spread the good news. Normally when God chooses a person, a vessel, He doesn't let that person know that he or she will have to suffer. But not so with Paul. God told Ananias to show Paul how much he would suffer for His name. And Paul never wavered one moment in fulfilling his call. In Philippians 4:12-13 he says, *"I know both how to be abased, and I know how to abound; everywhere and in all things I am instructed both to be full and to be hungry, both to abound and to suffer need. I can do all things through Christ which strengthens me."*

Affliction is an integral part of the process and we can't avoid it if we want to fulfill our mandate in the Lord. Sure we would all like to be treated like Queen Esther during the preparation process. After all, who wouldn't want to spend a year in a spa being pampered with oils and sweet perfumes and the likes? Who wouldn't like to be dressed in silk and sleep on the finest linen and ride in to purpose on a coach of ease? But in His eternal wisdom God has chosen the furnace as the place where we are purged and perfected. And in the long run, it is that perfection forged through hardship and trial that truly fit us to birth God's glorious purpose in our lives.

Jeremiah, Separated From The Womb

Jeremiah was separated and consecrated unto God in the office of a prophet from his mother's womb. When God told him of his separation and his assignment, Jeremiah brought up his age because he was a young man. When God is ready to separate you in preparation for the waiting room, He will not accept excuses such as, I'm too young, I'm too old, or I don't have enough money in the bank, or any such thing. God spoke to him and said, *"See, I have this day set thee over the nations and over the kingdoms, to root out, and to pull down, and to destroy, and to throw down, to build, and to plant*"(Jeremiah 1:10). The Lord probably showed him a vision of the things he would accomplish, but I don't believe he knew some of the obstacles he had to face because before long he was accusing God of deceiving him. In chapter 11:21 the Lord is speaking with him concerning His plan to deal with the men of Anathoth who were threatening to kill Jeremiah for prophesying in the name of the Lord. Anathoth was his home town and the men trying to kill him were priests. Jeremiah came from a priestly line and was commissioned by God to be a prophet. He came under attack from the religious people in his home town because of the word of the Lord in his mouth. There is a price to be paid when God separates you to speak His word. Like Nehemiah you will suffer attacks from enemies within and without. Religion is a word that actually means "to bind" and the religiosity in people will try to bind you and keep you from fulfilling what God has told you to do, and say what God has told you to say, but God has drawn a line and set a boundary and has decreed that His will shall be done in you and through you.

Abraham, Separated From His Home And Culture

When you search the scriptures you see many individuals whom God separated from that which was familiar in order to prepare them for purpose. Ur of the Chaldees was a thriving cultural city during the time of Abram. The inhabitants worshipped a moon god called Sin. It was from this same Ur of the Chaldees that God separated Abram to fulfill His purpose. God told him get away from his country, his kindred and his father's house to a land that He would show him. Abram's call gives us insight into the three things that God has to separate the believer from: 1) He has to separate him from the stagnation of familiarity—which is why He told him to leave his country; 2) He has to separate him from his old value system—that is why he had to separate from his kindred; and 3) He has to separate him from his father's house because God is now his new covering and spiritual head.

Why did God take a man from a land that worshipped a god called Sin and steeped in paganism? Because He doesn't look for perfect people, but for people to perfect. Don't think for a moment that there is any sin in your life, or that you come from too backward or immoral a place to be used by God. He is sovereign and He uses whomever He desires. He does not call us when we are perfect because then there would not be anyone to call. He separates us in our imperfection and prepares us for purpose so no man can boast that his works saved him. Thus all the honor and glory will go to God who is the only one worthy of praise.

On the other hand it can't be easy to separate yourself from all that is familiar and go to a land you "will be shown", not knowing what you will meet there. Abraham did not know where he was going when God called him, but He went because he **knew** who had called him. Stephen told the elders that, *"the God of glory appeared unto our father Abraham"* (Acts 7:2). Abram went because the God of glory had appeared to him. When the God of glory tells you to leave all that is familiar, move on because the land that He will show you will be far better than any land that you already occupy.

Many people are hindered from fulfilling God's purpose in their lives because of an unwillingness to separate from the familiar in order to embrace the promise. Many people are afraid to leave a church because great-grandma went there, grandma went there, and momma goes there. They feel it would be sacrilegious to leave their kindred. They are stuck in tradition and prefer to stay stuck even if there is no abiding presence there. They know there is a tug-and-pull in their spirit, but they are more concerned about the family tradition than what God wants to birth in them. There are people who will not allow God to separate them because they need to see the blueprint and the whole map of the land where God is sending them before they will go. But God will not give us a complete road map when He calls us to separate from the familiar because He expects us to walk by faith and trust Him to lead us. In any case, if He showed us the complete map we still might not go because there are "land mines" on the road and we may have to pass through "enemy territory".

When the Lord told Abram to leave his kindred, the call was for him to separate from his lineage, his native country, his culture. No matter how close you are to your family, no matter how much you love the place in which you live, God will not allow you to birth in that place, amongst that people, if it means your baby will continue in that same tradition that does not honor Him. God is interested in giving you a complete make-over in order to make you effective, and if He does not separate you from the familiar, the seed He plants in you may rot and die due to the stagnation of familiarity. God is pro-family but He cannot and will not unfold his promise in your life until you are willing to let Him launch you from your familial comfort zone. Jesus Himself told His disciples that if anyone is not willing to "hate"—disown, separate from—father or mother, they are not worthy of Him. (Luke 14:26). On another occasion when his mother and brethren were looking for Him, He declared, my mother and brethren are those who do the will of God. (See Mark 3: 30—32). Often times family ties can bog down the child of God who has been called to service and prevent her from fulfilling his call.

Lot, Separated At The Wrong Time And With The Wrong Motive

It is very important that we allow God to lead us in terms of the timing of our separation. Allowing our flesh to determine when we should move will lead to catastrophe. Genesis 13 records the story of the separation of Abram and his nephew Lot. The Bible says, *"Abram was very rich in cattle, in silver, and in gold. And he went on his journeys from the south even to Bethel, unto the place where his tent had been at the beginning, between Bethel and Hai"* (Genesis 13: 2-3). Abram and Lot were so wealthy that the land was not big enough to bear them both. Strife developed between the herdsmen of Abraham and the herdsmen of Lot. It is amazing how overflow and increase can bring strife. Abram suggested they separate and gave Lot the option of choosing first which land he would take. Lot chose the plain of Jordan because it was well watered and resembled the garden of the Lord. Lot left Abram and pitched his tent toward Sodom, which speaks for itself. The place looked good in the natural but he was not able to discern the wickedness which permeated the place. Abram was his covering and the one called by God, so Lot should have humbled himself and found a way to stay with Abram. His desire to have the best land caused him to wind up in a cesspool. Concerning the men of Sodom the Bible says, *"But the men of Sodom were wicked and sinners before the Lord exceedingly"* (Genesis 13: 13). The grass may look greener on the other side but you can wind up in quick sand if you are not able to discern what is beneath the surface.

Lot's life took a downward spiral once he separated from Abram. He was taken captive in a war between kings; he lost his wife when they were escaping the destruction of Sodom and Gomorrah. And the last we hear of him is when his two daughters got him drunk and slept with him. Separation is beneficial when it is orchestrated by the Lord and not the appetite of our flesh. Timing is crucial in every important decision of life. A dish taken out of the oven too soon will be undercooked, and one taken out too late will be overcooked. God's timing is impeccable and precise, so allow Him to determine when it is time for your next move. He will give you the confirmation and the peace concerning the move. Don't allow strife to be the catalyst that causes you to separate yourself ahead of His perfect timing for your life. Separation only works God's purpose of preparation when it is done under His guidance and with pure intentions. To separate for personal gain or through impatience can only lead to spiritual disaster. Lot's example should speak to all of us who believe the Lord is calling us to a different place of service. David said it best: *"Wait, I say, on the Lord."* (Psalm 27:14)

Ezekiel, Separated but Not Devastated

The Prophet Ezekiel was a servant of God who was separated from the land of his fathers and taken as a captive to a foreign land. But he did not spend his time murmuring and complaining. He kept his focus on God and in doing so he was able to transcend his captivity. He refused to allow his captivity to obscure his vision of God. While the other Israelites were sitting around singing songs of melancholy Ezekiel was experiencing great spiritual breakthroughs. Although he was among the captives he did not despair, nor lose sight of his heritage as a member of God's chosen people. In spite of his situation, he operated in the prophetic anointing. As a matter of fact, it was the very situation that opened the door for his promotion to the prophetic office. "*Now it came to pass in the thirtieth year, in the fourth month, in the fifth day of the month, as I was among the captives by the river of Chebar, that the heavens were opened, and I saw visions of God*" (Ezekiel 1:1) He didn't see his captivity, he saw God and accepted the call to lead his people back to a dependence and obedience to God. Ezekiel's separation was the vehicle for his promotion.

It will do the believer good to "take a page" from Ezekiel's book. If the believer is to find the promised promotion hoped for, if he is to give birth to the implanted seed, he must learn to see every difficult situation, and treat every obstacle and barrier with the same spirit Ezekiel did. The toughness of the situation is a barometer by which God measures those He seeks to promote. To quiver and quail is to prove yourself unfit and unworthy of the high calling of God. To look and see God in the difficult place, and to confidently walk through the "valley of the shadow of death" knowing that He is with you, is the most precious faith that God looks for in those He separates.

CHAPTER 2
WAITING

"I had fainted, unless I had believed to see the goodness of the LORD in the land of the living. Wait on the LORD: be of good courage, and he shall strengthen thine heart: wait, I say, on the LORD (Psalm 27: 13-14).

The heart of the psalmist speaks to our spirit as he emphasizes the importance of waiting on the Lord. According to the Life Application Bible, the theme of this psalm is: *"God offers help for today and hope for the future. Unwavering confidence in God is our antidote for fear and loneliness."* Waiting is never easy. We are not naturally inclined to appreciate delayed gratification because our human nature craves immediate satisfaction of our desires. Waiting can be frustrating, especially when the wait seems long and uncalled for and our dreams seem to have been derailed. David understood these challenges and difficulties inherent in the waiting process, so he encourages us to be of good courage and God will strengthen our heart [intellect, feelings, will]. No wonder he said that he would have fainted [given up in despair] had he not maintained his belief and expectation of seeing the goodness of the Lord in the land of the living. Thought precedes action so if we become discouraged in our hearts while we are waiting, we will get in the flesh and birth something that is not God ordained. David's experiences had taught him to wait on the Lord. Although anointed to be king at the age of sixteen, he did not actually become king until he was thirty. What was David doing between the ages of sixteen and thirty? He was in the waiting room being prepared through various tests and trials. His waiting room was the caves and wildernesses he lived in while running, when jealous King Saul was trying to kill him. David was no overnight-wonder-next-day-blunder because he had been tempered and forged through the rigors of the waiting room. From faithfully leading, providing for and protecting his sheep, to standing up to Goliath when all others were afraid, to not seeking to avenge himself on King Saul when he had the opportunity, his preparation for the kingship of Israel was full and complete.

Any serious search of the scriptures will show that any man of God who did anything of note for the Lord spent time in the waiting room. Take the Apostle Paul, who penned two thirds of the New Testament. In spite of having been separated him from his mother's womb for service, he did not go straight into his world-changing ministry when God called him on the Damascus road. Not at all! He spent three years alone with God in the waiting room Arabia and Damascus, so that God could prepare him for his calling.

Even Jesus had to be prepared for His public ministry. Although first sensing his special mission at twelve while in the Temple—He replies to his parents' remonstration about his delay in the Temple courts, "*did you not know that I must be about my Father's business?* (Luke 2:49)—, the Bible tells us that "*he went down with them and came to Nazareth, and was subject to them*" (Luke 2:51). In other words, he remained a willing and obedient son to his parents until his thirtieth birthday when he would officially begin his ministry. But that is not all. For after being baptized by His cousin John, he was lead of the Spirit into the wilderness to be tempted [Gr. *Peirazo*: tested, scrutinized, disciplined] by the devil. It didn't matter that the heavens opened and the Spirit of God descended upon Him like a dove. Nor did it matter that God spoke from Heaven and confirmed his call with the powerful affirmation: *"This is my beloved Son, in whom I am well pleased"* (Matt 3:17). (One would think that after such a great introduction and affirmation to public ministry, a person would be on easy street, but not so, for the very next thing that Jesus experiences is, forty days of enervating hunger and soul-wrenching temptation. Paul confirms this necessity of testing, of spending time in the waiting room, even for Jesus, the God Man, when he reminds the Hebrews that *"it was fitting for Him, for whom are all things and by whom are all things, in bringing many sons to glory, to make the author of their salvation perfect through sufferings...for in that he himself has suffered being tempted, he is able to aid those who are tempted."* (Hebrews 2: 10, 18).

Many people are told to accept Jesus as their personal savior, and then wait for the rapture. But the Lord has much more in store for us because salvation is not an end in itself, but the means to an end. The end is being conformed to the image and likeness of Jesus through a perfecting process. The perfecting process is a maturation process that involves trials, tribulations, and the furnace of affliction. It also involves the believer waiting on the Lord for preparation for their promotion to the next realm. Everything under God has a beginning, middle and end. The promise of God is the beginning, its fulfillment is the end, but there is a middle stage which is the developmental stage or the stage of preparation. It is in the middle that many of us experience differing degrees of difficulties, based on the level of the promise from God. The tests we take will always be commensurate with the level of our expected promotion. You can't expect happy meal trials when you desire **filet mignon** blessings.

I cannot impress upon you enough the importance of the preparation process in the waiting room. Jesus told His disciples that there are many mansions in His Father's house and He was going to prepare a place for them. The Kingdom of Heaven is a prepared place for a prepared people. It is the place where the bride will be presented to her groom, and she must be attired in the right clothing. This bride is a remnant that has been purged and purified to the point where there are no spots wrinkles, or blemishes. Queen Esther is a great example of the purification process a prospective bride needed to go through. She is a type of the church, the Bride of Christ. Her story paints a beautiful picture of the church's purification, and the believer's purification process in the waiting room as they await King Jesus. Just as Esther had been brought to Persia as a captive, in similar manner, the believer is born in sin and held captive by sin (see Psalm 51:5; John 8:34; Romans 7:24). And just as Esther had to be beautified, purified and prepared in order to become the king's wife, so, too, the church has to be prepared to spend eternity with Christ, her husband. Esther's preparation was detailed and elaborate because the bride could not go before the king with any spot, wrinkle, or blemish. In like manner, the Church has to be made pure and clean in order to consummate her spiritual marriage to Christ.

"So it came to pass, when the king's commandment and his decree was heard, and when many maidens were gathered together unto Shushan the palace, to the custody of Hegai, that Esther was brought also unto the king's house, to the custody of Hegai, keeper of the women. And the maiden pleased him, and she obtained kindness of him; and he speedily gave her things for purification, with such things as belonged to her, and seven maidens, who were meet to be given her, out of the king's house: and he preferred her and her maids unto the best place of the house of the women" (" (Esther 2:8, 9). Hegai represents a type of the Holy Spirit in that he gets the maidens prepared for the king in the same manner that the Holy Spirit gets the church ready for our King. There are habits and thought patterns that must be purged, and this is why the waiting room is necessary. It is where the Holy Spirit will work to bring about our total consecration and sanctification, and where we, as potential brides, must give the Holy Spirit complete access to our hearts and allow Him to do a

complete work in us. Because Esther pleased Hegai she was given three things: 1) He speedily gave her things for her purification, 2) she was given such things as belonged to her, and 3) She received seven maidens out of the king's house. Keep in mind that these were not just any maidens. These maidens were *meet to be given to her*, which means that they were particularly suitable for her. The Bride of Christ does not need to settle for just anything or anyone. God's desire is for us to have that which is particularly suitable for us. Not just any man. Not just any woman. Not just any job. God wants us to have His best!

Seven speaks of perfection and divine completion, so in essence she was given everything she needed to be purified to be a bride. The time frame for purification was twelve months. Twelve represents governmental perfection. It symbolizes God's perfect, divine accomplishment actively manifested. Six months was spent with oil of myrrh, six months was spent with sweet odors, and with other things for the purifying of the women. Myrrh was a principal ingredient in the holy anointing oil and formed part of the gifts brought by the wise men from the east who came to worship Baby Jesus. Oil is representative of the Holy Spirit and the anointing he empowers us to walk in. This anointing destroys the yokes that keep us bound.

Keep in mind Esther's time frame for preparation to be a bride consisted of six months spent with oil of myrrh, and six months spent with sweet odors. In Biblical numerology, six is the number which represents the flesh, the carnality of an unredeemed person whose life is not led by the Holy Spirit. No flesh can glory in the presence of the King so the "waiting room" is where the flesh is crucified and the "oil of myrrh" and other "sweet odors" can give the bride a pleasing odor to her groom. Jesus sweated drops of blood in the garden of Gethsemane. The word Gethsemane means olive press. The olive has to be crushed in order to get the oil; in like manner our flesh has to be crushed so the oil of His Spirit can flow in and through us. It must be crushed to the point where we cry; nevertheless, not my will Father, but thy will be done in and through us. The Lord desires to birth something great out of us, and this cannot be done through putrefying flesh. Like Aaron and his sons, we cannot go before the Lord without the anointing oil of the Holy Spirit. Resist the tendency to become idle and complacent while in the waiting room. Resist the encroachment of carnality on your mind from the world's system. We will miss our time of visitation if we are not prepared when the groom arrives.

The gospel writer Matthew gives an analogy comparing the Kingdom of Heaven to a certain king who made a marriage for his son. *"And when the king came in to see the guests, he saw there a man which had not on a wedding garment: And he saith unto him, Friend, how camest thou in hither not having a wedding garment? And he was speechless. Then said the king to the servants, Bind him hand and foot, and take him away, and cast him into outer darkness; there shall be weeping and gnashing of teeth"* (Matthew 22:11-13). This man was cast out not because he was uninvited, but because he had refused to wear the wedding garment provided. The wedding garment represented character development and sanctification. Being called is one thing, being sanctified another. That is why Christ warns that while many are called, only a few are chosen. Why? Because only a few choose to accept the rigors of preparation and the toils of development required to inherit the promise. Many want the crown but they refuse the cross. They want bright mansions but they won't pay the cost. In other words, they want to do things their way. But this parable warns us that the only way success in the spiritual is attained is through God's way.

I have first-hand experience of the Ishmaels that can and will be birthed when a spirit of anxiety causes us to step out of God's timing. There was a time when I felt that doors for ministry were not opening fast enough so I had to make things happen for myself. I didn't realize that it was God who had placed me in the waiting room in a holding pattern while He developed character and integrity in me. He would not allow my gifts and anointing to take me to places where my lack of character and integrity would cause me to be escorted out. At that particular time I had young children and the Lord wanted me to work a regular job and provide for them so they would have a strong foundation. However, all I could see was my desire to travel and preach the gospel. I wanted to be the next great evangelist and God's holding pattern surely didn't fit into my plans. Please don't get me wrong: my desire to preach flowed from a love for the gospel and the souls who needed to hear it, but there was this side of me that equated successful ministry with a busy schedule preaching before large crowds and this caused me to resist the waiting room experience.

Well, I fell flat on my face when I placed myself out there and hardly anyone called the "great evangelist" to preach. My bills piled up and my family suffered. I fell into a state of depression and spiritual confusion? Hadn't God placed His hand upon me and called me to ministry? Hadn't He rescued me from the ranks of Satan and commissioned me to bear the good news of His redemption? Then why was I languishing in anonymity and penury? I humbled myself before God and sought His wisdom and He gave me a great revelation. The great revelation was "get a J. O. B." You have a family to feed and a character to develop. You need the consistency of a regular job and the discipline of having to answer to authority. The Lord provided a job which provided for my family until my children were in college. He also sent me back into the waiting room of preparation where He dealt with my ambition and desire to be recognized through preaching, and my inclination to gauge ministerial success by what I saw other ministers doing.

In the beginning of the waiting period I was plagued with doubt that I would always labor for Him in the obscure place, that my ministry would be largely an unrecognized, insignificant work on the grand scale of things. But I gained peace after I realized that it is just as much an honor to witness to one individual on a street corner as it is to preach to a large crowd. The "waiting room" of humiliation and soul-searching is where I learned that principle. With peace and the acceptance of his timing for my life have come many opportunities to go out and minister. My promotion came through humility, patience and perseverance.

Are you willing to persevere in your waiting room while God takes you through your process of purification? Even if that waiting room is a maximum security prison? Or a half- way house where you wait for your transition back to a sense of normalcy? Will your faith allow you to see beyond the captivity of your body to the glorious freedom God is bringing to your spirit and mind? Or what if your waiting room is a body wracked by disease? Your doctors have pronounced you incurable and those around you are challenging your trust in God's power to heal you. Will you still hold on to your faith or will you listen to the doubters around you? The "waiting room" is usually not a pleasant place to be and many give in to despair because of its harshness. However, the spirit of worship and praise will transform any prison into a citadel of worship and praise, a tabernacle where there is a continual abiding presence of the King of glory. But this can only happen if you are willing to take your focus off your surroundings and present circumstance and place it on the glorious purpose God is working through your "waiting room" experience. Are you willing to "wait on the Lord"? (Psalm 27:14.)

Often the devil will attack our faith by bringing upon us tribulation and persecution during the waiting room experience. But we should not allow fear and doubt to get a foothold in our mind and cause us to become weary. In this, the three Hebrew young men, Shadrach, Meshach, and Abednego, can serve as a great example for us. They refused to let Nebuchadnezzar's threat of death in a fiery furnace cause them to lose their trust in God and bow to his image. Their response was: *"O Nebuchadnezzar, we are not careful to answer thee in this matter. If it be so, our God whom we serve is able to deliver us from the burning fiery furnace, and he will deliver us out of thine hand, O king. But if not, be it known unto thee, O king, that we will not serve thy gods, nor worship the golden image which thou hast set up"* (Daniel 3: 16-18). They did not abandon their allegiance to God in spite of the devil's attack, because they placed their trust in God and He entered the fire with them, preserving them from harm. The flames cannot harm the trusting child of God because he is greater than all and can conquer all. Not only that, God can bring His children, strengthened, renewed and exalted, out of these fiery experiences. Because of their faithfulness, God promoted them before the hosts of Babylon. Their waiting room experience led to their exaltation in the courts of Nebuchadnezzar.

Likewise, we must remember that no weapon, whether oppression, persecution, hardship, or trial, formed against us in the waiting room shall prosper. The Apostle Paul gives us great cause for rejoicing when he reminds us that "*...the sufferings of this present time are not worthy to be compared with the glory which shall be revealed in us"*... and ..."*who shall separate us from the love of Christ? Shall tribulation, or distress, or persecution, or famine, or nakedness, or peril, or sword...yet in all these things we are more than conquerors through Him [Christ] who loved us."* (Romans 8: 18, 35, 37). It is in these experiences that we mature to become more than conquerors. Yes, we are more than conquerors through Jesus Christ so we need not despair when the enemy bombards us with trials. In the waiting room, patience will be our strength. The victory over despair, despondency and fear will be ours if we hold fast our faith in God's promises and His methods, one of which includes the purifying of our souls and the strengthening of our characters through the flames of affliction. If we hold fast, the *stephanos* (victor's crown) will be ours and we shall ultimately inherit and occupy the Kingdom. See Revelation 2:10; 3:11.

Moses, Waiting And Learning

Moses stands head and shoulders above every other prophet in the Old Testament. God described Moses as a man who was faithful in his entire house. He contrasted the way he spoke with Moses with the manner in which He spoke to other prophets by saying, *"If there be a prophet among you, I the LORD will make myself known unto him in a vision, and will speak unto him in a dream, but not so my servant Moses whom I speak to face to face as a man speaketh to his friend"* (Numbers 12:6). But Moses did not get to that highly esteemed place with God overnight. His life consisted of three forty year periods: the first was spent as a prince in Egypt, where he tried, in his own humanity to liberate Israel and failed miserably. This was followed by another forty years in Midian, tending to his father-in-law's flocks. It was here that he had his encounter with God at the burning bush and was commissioned to do the very thing he had failed to do forty years before. His last forty years were spent leading Israel through the wilderness. This probably proved to be the greatest of all tests for Moses, and except for that time when he struck the rock instead of speaking to it, he passed with flying colors. No wonder God resurrected him and gave him the honor of encouraging Christ on the Mount of Transfiguration. Forty is the number of testing and probation, and three represents resurrection, divine completion and increase. So, one might say that Moses endured complete testing and probation and as a result was highly exalted above all other prophets, save Jesus. (It is interesting to note that two of God's greatest leaders in the Bible, Moses and David, both spent time leading sheep.)

The Apostle Paul in II Timothy 3:12 says, all who would live righteous in Christ Jesus will suffer persecution. God admonishes His children that they will be afflicted but the good news is that their affliction will not destroy them, but facilitate their anointing. As a matter of fact, when they are afflicted for the things of God, their affliction will actually cause them to grow. So be encouraged, servants of God, the affliction you endure in the waiting room will cause you to grow in stature if you yield to God's plan for your life. However in this season of affliction, saints of God, you will need what I call an *anointing of elasticity*—elasticity to be stretched by the afflictions but not broken by them. There is a purpose for the stretching: to develop spiritual thrust in those thus stretched. For just as the level of thrust in a rubber band is correlated to the level of its stretching—little stretch, little thrust, so too God wants to stretch you to the limit so that the resulting thrust and the momentum will propel you to the next level of purpose and to your divinely assigned place.

Job, Waiting With Patience

Perhaps the poster boy for maximum stretching in the waiting room, Job went through a time of affliction and testing very few will ever be called to face. Everything he owned was wiped out—his children, his livestock, his home. He literally went from being the richest man in the east to sitting in ashes and scraping himself with a potsherd—part of a broken clay pot—because of the sore boils all over his body. His wife was the one person left alive in his family and instead of speaking words of life, she spoke words of discouragement—whatever happened to, "in sickness and in health, for richer or poorer till death do us part." She came to him and asked, *"Dost thou still retain thine integrity? Curse God, and die."* (Job 2:9). But Job not only held on to his integrity—Hebrew: *tummah,* singleness of purpose, innocence—he waited patiently on the Lord for his healing and restoration.

Job's three friends were not much comfort to him either. Although Eliphaz, Bildad, and Zophar were men of wisdom who had a deep understanding of doctrine, they misjudged the reason for his suffering. They assumed that his suffering was caused by some great sin in his life. They judged, accused, and debated with him concerning his condition, never once uttering a word of comfort, encouragement or support. Their presence actually made Job's trial greater, just as there are people in your life who, although well-meaning, make your trials in the waiting room more difficult because they misjudge your circumstance and the outworking of God's plan in your life. You don't need a doctrinal theologian when you are struggling in the waiting room; you need a person with compassion that has a word from the Lord. Each time Job sank into a valley of doubt, his firm knowledge of God's justice and mercy would lift him up to heights of faith. At one point he even exclaimed: "*For He knows the way I take, when He has tried [tested] me I shall come forth like gold.*" (Job 23:10). Job also realized that his remaining faithful through the test would be the key to the outworking of God's plan in his life, for he continues: "*My foot has held fast to His steps; I have kept His way and not turned aside. I have not departed from the commandment of His lips; I have treasured the words of His mouth more than my necessary food.*" (Job 23:11, 12). Eventually, God would rebuke his friends for their attitude towards Job during his trial and He sent them to Job for him to intercede on their behalf. And to show His ultimate favor to Job, he made him even richer than before. Because of his faithfulness and patience, Job's experience has been a source of encouragement, strength and an example of patient endurance to countless saints as they go through their purification and preparation in the waiting room. A point of note is that Job came out of the waiting room a better person. His trial not only vindicated God's confidence in Him and proved that Job was, indeed, an upright man, but it also polished Job's character and gave him a better, more accurate perspective of his own weaknesses and God's greatness and love. In other words, Job has been lifted to new heights in his own spiritual experience, just as much as he became God's instrument to reveal the mysteries of suffering. Nobody comes out of the waiting room as he went in.

The waiting room changes you as surely as it prepares you for promotion.

Joseph, Waiting And Trusting

Joseph is another individual whose life paints a portrait of patience while enduring trials in the waiting room. Joseph was hated by his brothers because he was his father's favorite. The Bible says, *"Now Israel loved Joseph more than all his children, because he was the son of his old age: and he made him a coat of many colors"* (Genesis 37:3). In those days everyone wore a coat or a cloak to keep them warm, to bundle up belongings for a journey or to wrap babies. Most cloaks were very plain, but it appears Joseph's coat was similar in type to the ones worn by royalty. I am sure his brothers were not enamored with the fact that he was his father's favorite, but the situation between them worsened when Joseph dreamed that his parents and his brothers would bow before him in homage. He was 17 at the time and his youthful immaturity no doubt caused him to boast about his dream. His maturity would come in the waiting rooms of the pit, Potiphar's house and the prison. He could not be promoted to the palace until he experienced this three step process.

His brothers were still chafing over a negative report Joseph had given his father about them when they saw him coming through the fields to look for them. "Let's get rid of this dreamer", they said as he approached them, initially intending to kill him. However, after some hasty negotiation among themselves, they threw him into a pit and then sold him to some Ishmaelites for twenty pieces of silver. He faced a 30-day journey through the desert, probably chained hand and foot. What a baptism of fire for this hitherto "special son", who was now facing the unknown under the most inhospitable conditions.

The Ishmaelites sold Joseph to Potiphar, an official in Pharaoh's court. But the hand of the Lord was on Joseph and he found favor in Potiphar's house. When Joseph took up his work at Potiphar's house, he was a slave and an alien. First, he became a personal attendant to the Egyptian officer. When Potiphar found him alert, quick, and trustworthy, and saw that the Lord was with him (v. 3), he set him over the entire establishment as his trusted overseer. In his new position Joseph was responsible for every detail of the management of the house, with one exception: As a foreigner, he could not see to the preparation of food. He was appointed steward of Potiphar's house not because of some special divine blessing, but because he was faithful in discharging his duties. In other words, God blessed him *through his diligence*, not apart from it. "*What ever your hands find to do, do it with all your might.*" (Ecclesiastes 9:10; see also Matthew 25: 20, 21). Somehow I think Joseph never murmured or complained but kept his composure and trusted in the Lord his God. He accepted the reality of his situation but did not allow it to dictate how he would behave. He most likely felt that he would never see his beloved father, Jacob, again, but he would act like a true son of promise. He would hold on to his father's God like never before, and he would make it through this. He decided he would not despair, but would have faith and patience.

But, for every level of promotion there is a different test. Realizing that hardship wasn't working with Joseph, the enemy switched gears. He would try flattery and sensuality where hardship and affliction didn't work. Now that Joseph was a steward in Potiphar's house, enjoying the better things of life, Satan decided to destroy him through lust and ease. He unleashed Potiphar's wife on him. *"Now it came to pass that after these things that his master's wife cast longing eyes on Joseph, and she said, "Lie with me."* (Genesis 39: 7). Yet Joseph remained true to principle and would not let himself be seduced by Potiphar's wife (See verses 8—10.) Her seductive approaches rebuffed, Potiphar's wife tried one last desperate attempt to force Joseph to have sex with her. But when even that failed, she finally accused him of rape because she was so embarrassed and angered by his rejection of her sexual attempts. I wonder how many individuals are languishing in prison falsely accused of rape by a spurned suitor. Thanks be to Christ that DNA testing is exonerating many that are innocent.

Potiphar put him in prison, but even there the Lord continued to bless him. He found favor with the keeper of the prison because he refused to let bitterness and despair gain the upper hand. Like he had done at Potiphar's house, Joseph put his best foot forward, so to speak, and he was made supervisor of the prisoners. Prison is not exactly the best waiting room to be in but to those who make God their guide; the prison can become a place of breakthroughs, just like it was for Joseph. So, whatever place you may find yourself in; find a way to use it as an opportunity for ministry. You might be reading this from an actual prison or from some prison of the mind, but don't allow your environment to determine the level of your effectiveness or lack thereof. If you experience *a setback*, don't take *a step back*; know that God is working on your *comeback.*

When the king's butler and baker were thrown into prison, and dreamed, Joseph was able to give the interpretation. The interpretation for the baker was not pleasant because he would lose his head, but the butler would be restored to his position as cupbearer to the king. Joseph made a request of the butler, "... *remember me when it is well with you, and please show kindness to me; make mention of me to Pharaoh, and get me out of this house" (Genesis 40:14).* One can only imagine the intensity—so well known to any who has been in the waiting room, awaiting God's deliverance—of Joseph's emotion as he makes his request known to the butler. However, the butler forgot about Joseph once he had been reinstated.

Like Job, you may not have received much comfort from your spouse in your crisis; your spouse might be the cause of your crisis. Your friends might be more critical and judgmental than encouraging. Or like Joseph, you might have suffered at the hands of siblings, been wrongfully accused and even neglected by those who promised to help you. But know that God has not forgotten you. He is not slack concerning his promises. The waiting room can be a place of renewal and refreshing and a classroom of learning. *"He giveth power to the faint; and to them that have no might he increaseth strength. Even the youths shall faint and be weary, and the young men shall utterly fall: But they that wait upon the LORD shall renew their strength; they shall mount up with wings as eagles; they shall run, and not be weary; and they shall walk, and not faint" (Isaiah 40:29-31).*

God had not forgotten about Joseph or his plight. He did not allow the butler to remember the request because it was not time for Joseph to be released. Besides, he wanted Joseph, and us, to be clear about the fact that *"... promotion cometh neither from the east, nor from the west, nor from the south. But God is the judge: he putteth down one, and setteth up another" (Psalms 75:6-7).* But when it came time for his release God gave Pharaoh a dream that neither the magicians nor the wise men of Egypt could interpret. At that point the butler remembered how his dream had been interpreted in the prison, and informed Pharaoh that he had met a young Hebrew man in prison, who was able to interpret his dream. When Pharaoh heard the report about Joseph, he immediately sent for him. Joseph's *kairos* [opportune, seasonable, appointed] time had arrived.

Joseph told Pharaoh about the famine that would hit Egypt and how to prepare for it. The Bible says Joseph's advice was good in the eyes of Pharaoh and in the eyes of all his servants. Pharaoh was impressed, clearly discerning a different, superior spirit in Joseph and he exclaimed, *"Can we find such a one as this, a man in whom is the Spirit of God?"* (Genesis 41:37). Satisfied that he had found the best candidate in Joseph, Pharaoh promoted him and set him over all the land of Egypt and its "famine relief" efforts. It is fascinating to note that it was the revelation of his dream to his family that set Joseph on course to the pit, Potiphar's house and the prison, but it is the interpretation of the butler's dream that opened the door to his promotion to the palace. The very thing that appears to be problematic for us is the very thing the Lord will use to promote us; "And we know that all things work together for good to them that love God, to them who are called according to His purpose." (Romans 8:28). God wants to take ordinary men and women like you and me, mold us in the waiting room and then use us to do the extraordinary. The question is, "will we allow Him to do His work, in His way and in His time?"

This same Joseph who spent time in a pit, was sold into slavery, accused of rape, and thrown into prison, is now in the palace. Yes, my friends, this same Joseph is able to provide food for the brothers who hated him, when famine hit the land. He does not seek revenge on his brothers when the opportunity presents itself. In fact he tells them, "*God sent me before you to preserve posterity for you in the earth and to save your lives by a great deliverance*" (Genesis 45:7). Joseph is a model of patience and understanding in the waiting room, and forgiveness after he gets out. When the Lord God Almighty delivers you out of your waiting room, don't seek revenge or harbor ill will and animosity towards those who hurt, forgot and neglected you. Be a blessing to them by showing forgiveness.

It is interesting to note that as a brash, boastful 17-year old, Joseph described his dream to his brothers by using words like *I* and *my*. His words to them were, *"Hear, I pray you, this dream which I have dreamed" (Genesis 37:6).* He does not appear to realize that it was the Lord showing him how he would be promoted. Contrast this, however, with how he speaks to the butler, the baker and Pharaoh about their dreams and interpretation after his sojourn in the pit, Potiphar's house and the prison. When the butler and the baker told him there was no one to interpret their dreams, his response was, *"Do not interpretations belong to God?" (Gen 40:8).* When Pharaoh told him his dream, he responded by saying, *"God hath shewed Pharaoh what he is about to do." (Gen. 41:25).* In the crucible of the waiting room you mature and grow more humble and less self-reliant.

Samson, Waiting But Unaware

It must be noted that although God purges us through affliction and prepares us for promotion through hardships, some of the trials we endure in the waiting room may be a direct result of self-inflicted wounds caused by a deficiency in our character. These character flaws hinder us from greatness and are the avenues through which the enemy can trip us up and short-circuit God's glorious plan for our lives. And until these flaws are remedied, our stay in the waiting room *will be prolonged.* As a matter of fact, we will remain in the waiting room long past the season that we should have been out; and we will endure trials way over what was initially necessary to prepare us for our promotion. Such a waiting room experience is usually much more difficult to bear because, like the father who paces impatiently in the hospital waiting room wondering why his wife has not delivered their baby as yet, since her time was due, the waters had broken and labor pains had begun, we look around and realize that we, ourselves, were due, and the conditions for our promotion were ripe, and we had begun to see signs of the fulfillment of our promise, and yet, here we are, still "childless", still groaning and pushing, and anticipating, but bringing forth…nothing.

Samson (Judges 13—16) represents the many of us who are still in the waiting room, suffering and groaning because of those self-inflicted wounds of character weakness. Samson was a mighty man, a judge of Israel, born miraculously for the great task of delivering God's people from Philistine oppression. In spite of the divinely appointed circumstances of his birth, upbringing and calling, he lost his covering and his vision because he did not get deliverance from a spirit of lust and presumption. Though gifted above all other men with strength, he was weak to the wiles of a prostitute named Delilah, and he languished in a Philistine prison for many seasons because he rested his head in the lap of a woman whose very name meant *languishing.*

He was a Nazarite from birth, a testament that his life would be one of complete and unreserved dedication to God and His purposes. His abstemious lifestyle and uncut hair were to be external symbols of his unwavering dedication to Yahweh who was the source of his strength. But Samson either chose to ignore this fact, or he had become so used to doing his own thing, he had forgotten. In either case, he had gotten so used to getting in and out of trouble—which usually involved the Philistines, their women and drunkenness, he took it for granted that no matter what, he could always "take care of business." It was this impetuousness, this same presumptuous spirit, this same licentiousness, that lead him to sleep in his enemy's bed, drink of her wine, taste her kisses, luxuriate in her caresses and lay on her knees, instead of leading his people and doing God's business. But she, with undistracted focus, and undeterred determination was unrelenting in her quest to find the source of his strength; after all, the lords of the Philistines had promised her a tidy sum if she could. And what about you, my brother, my sister? Are you, like Samson, "sleeping with the enemy", willfully ignorant of the fact that the enemy's only purpose is to kill, steal and destroy God's purpose for your life; that he is using your very character weaknesses and flaws to defeat you and keep you in the waiting room?

And her persistence finally paid off because the Bible says, *"And it came to pass, when she pressed him daily with her words, and urged him, so that his soul was vexed unto death;"* (Judges 16:16). She wore him down and he revealed all his heart to her. Once he exposed his heart to her she summoned the Lords of the Philistines. Then she put him to sleep on her knees, and while he slept she had a man shave off the seven locks of his head (Judges 16:19). When they found Sampson he was asleep on Delilah's knees. Knees not only speak of worship, they also speak of submission and surrender. What a horrible way for a man of God to be overtaken by his enemies: sound asleep on the knees of a harlot instead of being on his knees praying and seeking God. When Delilah told him that the Philistines were upon on him he awoke from his sleep and said, *"I will go out as at other times before, and shake myself" (Judges 16:20),* and he confidently went out to meet the Philistines as he had always done before. However, this time the Philistines easily overpowered and bound him because Samson had already been bound, gagged and blinded long before they had come upon him. But he, tragically, didn't know his strength was gone, and the Lord had departed from him. He thought everything was still the same. He thought it was business as usual, but mercy and grace had retired for the season and judgment had come to replace them. And like Samson, there are many servants of God moving in their own strength, unaware that the presence of the Lord has departed, unaware that judgment has come and unaware that they are about to be placed in some dire straits where they will either learn the lessons neglected or be ultimately cast aside as unfit for service.

The sobering thought about Samson is that in spite of his prodigious strength and divinely appointed calling, he lacked the one thing that would have given him true success and glorified God: self discipline. Like so many others who lack self discipline, Samson's life was mediocre when it could have been great, his accomplishments tainted by his moral and spiritual failures. The testimony of Samson's life is also a vindication of God's method of purging, pruning, purifying and preparing us before promoting us. Unlike Moses, whose character was forged in the suffocating heat of the wilderness; or David, whose courage and sense of purpose were steeled as he protected his sheep from predators; or the Three Hebrew Young Men, who were tested and refined in the crucible of the fiery furnace; or Paul, once blinded by his arrogance but humbled by the revelation of Christ himself as he waited in silence and soul-searching those years in Arabia (see Galatians 1:14—17), Samson went straight from his mother's bosom, so to speak, into ministry. He treated it with the same boyish, immature and selfish attitude that usually characterizes one who has not learned through hardship, the trial and tests or the "discipline of effective service and greatness." Do you find yourself angry because God has you in the waiting room longer than you think you should be? Are you overly eager to get out and get going? Can you hardly wait to be on the front lines? Do you feel that God is delaying your release into your perceived calling and mission? Then I would remind you to contemplate the life of Samson and wait on the Lord. Like the hymn writer, humbly pray, "*Have thine own way, Lord, have Thine own way. Thou art the Potter, I am the clay.*" And then let patience have her perfect way in you (James 1:4)

The first thing the Philistines did was they put his eyes out. They took away his vision because he had already lost sight of who he was and what he was supposed to do. Samson was plunged into the darkness of blindness because his eyes had become a major distraction, leading him to walk away from the light. In truth, he was the embodiment of Jesus' foreboding words: "*The eyes are the light of the body and if that light becomes darkness, how great the darkness.*" (Matthew 6:22, 23) Then they brought him down to Gaza, their "fortified place" where he was bound with fetters of brass, cast into a dungeon, chained to a mill and forced to grind grain. Ironically, the grindstone was circular so in spite of his constant movement, he was simply going around in circles, forever moving but staying in the same place. How humiliating to see the mighty deliverer of Israel reduced to this pitiful sight; to see a man born for greatness, living out his days in the mundane. Do you recognize yourself, dear reader, in Samson's predicament? Have you also found yourself in a "fortified place", chained, as it were to a circular stone, where, in spite of all your activities and efforts to the contrary, you find yourself going nowhere? Then perhaps you too, like Samson, have been brought to this place so that you might learn what it really means to "wait on the Lord" (Psalm 37: 34), and to "renew your strength in the Lord" (Isaiah 40: 31).

Samson's prison would become his waiting room where he would begin again to see and be what God had preordained. The Philistines praised their god Dagon for delivering Samson into their hands, just like those around you may praise their "connections" for their having advanced over you, or their maneuvering for having cost you that position. Little do they realize, just like the Philistine didn't realize, that it was all part of God's chastening process whereby He might make us *partakers of His holiness*...that we might...*yield the peaceable fruit of righteousness of those trained by it* [chastening] (see Hebrews 12:5—11). But hallelujah! God doesn't place us in the dungeon to leave us there. He will not always chide, nor will He keep His wrath forever, for the Bible tells us, *"Howbeit the hair of his head began to grow again after he was shaven"* (Judges 16:22). O, yes, my friends, the restoration of the visible sign of God's covenant with Samson was the token that God had not forsaken Samson, just like He will not forsake you if you "*do not despise the chastening of the Lord, nor be discouraged when you are rebuked by Him*" (Hebrews 12:5). So if you have found yourself in a place of affliction because of some bad decisions or unconquered character defects, don't give up because the Lord will cause your strength to return even in the midst of the trial if you come to repentance and turn back to Him. After having his hair shaved, his eyes plucked out, and his ego "checked at the door" and burnt up in the flames of his humiliation, there was no more self left in Samson, only a sense of his own unworthiness. After being forced to grind in the prison house and to entertain his captors, Samson recognized his complete dependence upon God, his refuge and strength. So when the Philistines brought him out of the prison house to make a mockery of him, little did they realize—to their own undoing, that his strength had returned and that God would use him one more time in a final display of strength and dependence that would reverberate throughout the ages to come. As Samson was lead to the pillars that held up the temple of Dagon, he cried out to God, *"O Lord GOD, "remember me, I pray thee, and strengthen me, I pray thee, only this once, O God, that I may be at once avenged of the Philistines for my two eyes" (Judges 16:28).* And in this, his finest moment, he killed more Philistines than he had done when he had his strength and his vision.

Samson's end was tragic in the sense that he died with the Philistines, but it serves as a lesson book to us that even though the Lord may redeem us and use us once again, there are many times when He will not save us from the consequences of our folly and we will have to live with those consequences for the rest of our lives, never quite achieving the fullness of the purpose God had for us. There are times when the Ishmaels that we birth will live on to torment and harass us. There will be scars that remain to remind us of our presumptuousness, immaturity and impatience. How necessary then that we learn to wait on the Lord and learn the lessons of humility and patience. How vital, too, that we develop a spirit of immediate repentance so that we might stem the tide of woe that may accompany our recklessness. Waiting in trust and patience is never easy, but it is never as painful and grueling as chastening. Nor will it produce such destructive fruit as Samson's, or our immaturity and impetuosity.

Waiting And Ready

Preparation for greatness is never easy. It takes time because God has to get us ready to handle the challenges we will face in the next dimension. God knows the ending from the beginning. He has a panoramic view, and that means He sees everything at once. We, on the other hand, see through a glass that is dimly lit (I

Corinthians 13: 12), so we must trust God's timing for our lives.

There are many individuals who have left ministries before the men and women under whom they were being nurtured had birthed them. They felt they were sitting too long waiting for their breakout so they left prematurely and started works that may not have been ordained or sanctioned by God. The result was that they found themselves in a position where they were ill-equipped to handle the onslaught that came against them because instead of being sent, they just packed up and went.

On the flip side, there are many individuals who have been, and are being held back by leaders who refuse to release them into their own ministry. These leaders have come to rely so heavily on the gifting of these individuals, they are afraid that a vacuum will be created if they are released. As difficult as it may be for "the parent" to see the child leave home, they should remember that resentment will build in the individual if they have to sit too long. For this reason, many qualified ministers are languishing in houses of worship, bitter in spirit, because they know it is their time to go forth but are being held back. Many of them have been forced to break away from the local assembly because leadership refused to bless them and release them. Jesus trained His disciples and when the time was ripe He released them with a commission to go into all the world and make disciples. Likewise, a good leader will be able to discern the time when a son or daughter should be birthed out. Such a leader recognizes that holding them past their release point will hinder them because the very womb that protects and incubates a baby can endanger that baby's life if the baby stays there past delivery time.

Are you a believer who has served faithfully in your local assembly and sense the time of your birthing is near? Do you feel yourself getting anxious or discouraged because of the length of time you've waited? Do not allow anxiety to draw you into the flesh. *"Be careful for nothing; but in everything by prayer and supplication with thanksgiving let your requests be made known unto God. And the peace of God, which passeth all understanding, shall keep your hearts and minds through Christ Jesus"* (Philippians 4: 6-7). God keeps in perfect peace the mind that is stayed upon Him by imparting the anointing of the Holy Spirit. According to Hebrews 12:2, Jesus was able to endure the cross and despise the shame because of the joy that was set before Him. Do not spend a great deal of time focusing on the time that appears to be lost. The Lord is able to redeem the time. Get into praise mode and thank Him for what He has already done while you await the fulfillment of your divine destiny.

Prayer, supplication and thanksgiving must be active ingredients in your life while in the waiting room. Remember, it was the psalmist's belief that he would see the goodness of the Lord *in the land of the living* that kept him from fainting. Although he did not see it at the time, his faith gave him an assurance that he would not die before it was manifested. You must have the same faith and belief. A friend of mine told me, "You must see it before you see it."

HOW LONG, O LORD, BEFORE YOU ANSWER?
(A word to my dearly beloved sisters in the waiting room of singleness and expectancy)

Every Christian, at some point in his or her journey, spends time—some long, others short—in the waiting room. For instance, there might be someone waiting for an organ transplant, let's say, a kidney, or a liver or a heart. And we would all agree that this is critical, of vital importance—most of us would even drop all we are doing to help this individual with the malfunctioning kidney pray for a donor organ, because we can sympathize with his or her frequent and difficult trips to dialysis and the suffering such a condition would entail while waiting for a replacement kidney to become available. But what about the person who might be waiting for a new job or a house? We might consider those as optional requests, not of vital importance. But even if others consider what we wait for as minor, to those of us doing the waiting, it is very important. Like the many wonderful Christian women waiting on the Lord for the right husband to come along so they can start a family. Or those who may already have a loving husband but are kept from the joy of motherhood due to an inability to conceive. There are those who would disparage such concerns as being unworthy of the sold-out-for-Christ Christian woman, but who can tell another what should be the *desires of her heart*? (See Proverbs 3:5.) As they hear their biological clock ticking and the windows of opportunity close a bit tighter with each passing day, can you empathize with their disconsolation, as they cry out to their Master, "Why me?" After all, they have kept themselves for many years from fornication while waiting on a man of God. Yet they see other women being proposed to— many of them not as attractive, anointed, or as spiritual as they are— while they remain on the shelf, so to speak. (And, of course, their frustration is made worse by the single, church playboys who love the attention they get from the plethora of desperate women seeking to get married, but who have no intention of committing to any of them.) What is a sister to do?

For the Christian woman living the sanctified life, the situation can seem very bleak indeed. Many brothers are either locked down in prison, gay, effeminate, hanging out on the corner with the 'fellas' or simply not interested in marriage. Many sisters, in a bid to "make it happen" allow the adversary entrance into the "waiting room" where he entices them to settle for any man, even the unsaved: "Forget about the Scriptural injunction about being "unequally yoked. You can always study the Bible with him and lead him to Christ afterwards. He is not as bad as people make it look, and you can always change him once you get married. Besides, look at the great qualities he possesses…much better than many of the men in the church. In any case, God understands your loneliness and He wants you to be comforted..." The spiritual self-brainwashing goes on and on until they find themselves in bed, forming strong soul ties through their sexual encounter and intellectual and emotional stimulation, with a man not their husband, not of their faith and not intending to walk this Christian pathway with them. Like Abram and Sarai, they get so tired and discouraged from the years of waiting, they take matters into their own hands. They overlook warning signs, and disregard the still small voice speaking to their spirit, warning them of the precipice that lies ahead, admonishing them that many men will go as far as to go to church with a sister because they know she will be more inclined to date them if it appears they are moving in a Godly direction. They put blinders on and are unable to discern the wolf dressed in sheep's clothing.

And just like Abram and Sarai, these sisters must live with the Ishmaels that they have birthed: either being strung along for years with thinly veiled promises of marriage, or living many years of misery in a marriage not ordained, nor blessed by God. For once the wolf gets what he wants; he will take off the sheep's clothing and revert back to his true form. Many women have found themselves living with an abusive monster, a Jekyll and Hyde character who started to abuse them once the honeymoon was over.

Keeping the flesh under control might seem like an impossibility and the enticement of companionship might seem too strong to resist, but if these beloved sisters in Christ could only hear some of the horror stories experienced by others, they would realize that living single with Christ is much better than living in a bitter and heavy yoke of marriage.

Waiting: Fighting The Good Fight Of Faith

Waiting is difficult because, according to Bishop Noel Jones, "it messes with our faith." The anxiety of waiting is exacerbated by the fact that we live in a "microwave" world where we want things to happen now. We are not a people who have been conditioned to wait. From the time we break forth from our mother's womb, we demand immediate attention, and we know how to get it. Everything about our society speaks of speed and quickness. We travel on the information super highway where we get our information at a moment's notice. Satellites allow us to stay in our living rooms and witness events transpiring in other nations in real time. We use instant messaging because email isn't fast enough. We place our foods in microwave ovens to be heated and wait impatiently for those two minutes to be up. And if you are like me, sometimes you stop it before the allotted time, only to find out that the top is warm but the inside is cold, and have to put it back in. We want cars that go from zero to sixty in a matter of seconds.

As believers we experience difficulties when we try to apply this paradigm to the Kingdom of God. We desire to move at supersonic speed, but based on experience, it appears that God is not enamored with the fast lane. God appears to like the slow roast as opposed to microwave cooking. Here is our challenge, how do we wait on the Lord without birthing an Ishmael? This can only be done if we continue to look at the "waiting room"—the period between the promise and the fulfillment— as a place of purpose and preparation for our kingdom assignment here on earth. This is "the place" where the adversary visits us with his clouds of doubt that make us feel that the Lord has forgotten us. This is "the place" where we are either lead to presumption or despondency. And this is where the Ishmaels of our lives are birthed.

The Apostle Peter said, *"Forasmuch then as Christ hath suffered for us in the flesh, arm yourselves likewise with the same mind: for he that hath suffered in the flesh hath ceased from sin."* (1 Peter 4:1). Peter uses the Greek word *hoplizo* for *arm* and it means to equip with weapons. Christ suffered in the flesh so that we don't have to be held captive by the flesh and its lustful passions. We must equip ourselves for warfare by "arming ourselves" with the knowledge of the enemy's tactics and weapons." ... *We are not ignorant concerning his devices* (2 Corinthian 2:11). In this spiritual war we cannot use carnal weapons to defeat the devil. Paul wrote, "*For the weapons of our warfare are not carnal, but mighty through God to the pulling down of strong holds; Casting down imaginations, and every high thing that exalteth itself against the knowledge of God, and bringing into captivity every thought to the obedience of Christ"* (2 Corinthians 10:4-5). The Apostle didn't say the weapons of *his* warfare, but the weapons of *our* warfare. No believer is exempt, because there are no pacifists, or conscientious objectors in this war. The level of attack you face is always based on the level of the revelatory word God has placed in you and the level of that word you are operating in.

Paul told the Corinthians that the messenger of Satan was sent to buffet him lest he should be exalted above measure. The word buffet means *to beat to a pulp*. This happened because of the abundance of revelation that he received and walked in. He uses the definite article *the messenger* because the word messenger in the Greek is *aggelos* and in Paul's case the *aggelos* was a high ranking demon. This is not the kind of war where the enemy launches long range missiles at us; on the contrary, this war is up close and personal. Paul said, *"For we wrestle not against flesh and blood, but against principalities, against powers, against the rulers of the darkness of this world, against spiritual wickedness in high places" (*Ephesians 6:12). The New American Standard Bible says, *"For our struggle—hand to hand combat—is not against flesh and blood."*

He doesn't say, for *I* wrestle or struggle, but *we,* because the attack is against the body of Christ. Don't feel isolated in the waiting room of your trial as if the enemy has targeted you alone; you are being attacked along with every other member of the Church Jesus is building. Identify the spirit behind the thing you are wrestling with. Satan will also use people to try to oppress and perplex us. We must fully clothe ourselves in the full armor of God if we are to survive the onslaught of the enemy. Stop looking at flesh and blood; stop focusing on people and discern the spirit causing them to act the way they do. Wife, take your eyes off your husband. Husbands take your eyes off your wife; attack the spirit that is attacking them and using them.

The devil will do anything to get us to act independently of God—from persecution, to hardships to temptation. He knows he has no room to operate as long as we are being led by the Holy Spirit, so he entices us with speculative questions hoping to get us to begin questioning the plain word of God and thus create doubt in our minds. No wonder Peter called him a roaring lion because he is relentless in his attack against our minds, to drive a wedge of doubt or discouragement into our spirits. And once he sees an opening, he pounces immediately to set up strongholds in our minds, which then "tune into" and "lock onto" fleshly things.

He loves to attack us in the areas where we are awaiting the fulfillment of God's promises. His sole intent is to get us to take matters into our own hands and run ahead of God. One of his devices is to get us to take our eyes off God and focus on what we don't have, and what others have. The Bible assures us that God hastens His word to perform it because "*He is not slack concerning His promises as some count slackness*" (2 Peter 3:9). If it came from the Mouth of God then it must come to pass in your life. Don't believe the lies of the devil when he tries to convince you otherwise because you've spent a long time waiting on the fulfillment of the prophetic word spoken over you. Anything spoken to you in the waiting room that is contrary to what God has promised is a lie from the devil, and you must cast it out immediately. Don't allow it to take root in your mind or it will sprout and produce something carnal in your life.

Remember Job? Remember how difficult his waiting room experience was? And yet he was sustained. Job said, *"all the days of my appointed time will I wait, till my change come."* (Job 14:

14) He knew it would happen. He just had to wait patiently for it. So, too, the Christian must wait in watchful praying and flesh-crucifying fasting. Many people birth Ishmaels in the waiting room because they get tired "sitting around" waiting for God. (They think they are waiting on God when in actuality God is waiting for them. Waiting for them to fast and pray. Waiting on them to sow the seeds of their faith into the soil of perseverance, humility, watchfulness and obedience. Waiting for them to mature in their faith and character so they can handle the promotion promised, the ministry bestowed.) But without spiritual maturity, most Christians would make shipwreck of their faith and experience if taken to the dizzying heights of prosperity, success and notoriety that God desires to bestow on them. Revelation 12:2 describes a woman being with child and crying, travailing in birth and pained to be delivered. Godly growth comes at a price: the level of travailing we are willing to endure in order to give birth.

Sometimes it appears that individuals who don't have the same level of kingdom commitment are getting breakthroughs, while we fast, pray, and serve the Lord in the beauty of holiness with minimal success. Sometimes the unbeliever appears to be on a course of supersonic acceleration while the life of the believer seems to be one long waiting for one thing or another. The psalmist Asaph was perplexed by this, and out of his frustration he wrote, *"Truly God is good to Israel, even to such as are of a clean heart. But as for me, my feet were almost gone; my steps had well nigh slipped. For I was envious at the foolish, when I saw the prosperity of the wicked."* (Psalm 73:1-3). He knew that God was good to Israel, but he almost backslid when he saw the wicked prospering. As you wait on the Lord for a particular blessing, are you becoming envious as you see worldly people prospering? Be encouraged, God has not forgotten His promises concerning you. Asaph went on to say, *"When I thought to know this, it was too painful for me; Until I went into the sanctuary of God; then understood I their end. Surely thou didst set them in slippery places: thou castedst them down into destruction. How are they brought into desolation, as in a moment! they are utterly consumed with terrors"* (Ps 73:16-19). Yes, it was in the sanctuary that his spiritual eyes were opened to the realities his physical eyes could not discern. The sanctuary [Hebrew: *miqqedash* (mik-ked-awsh'), a consecrated or holy place] is the place of closeness and intimacy with God Himself. It is the place where man can come away from the stresses, pleasures, distractions and confusion of the world and receive the revelation of God. It is in the sanctuary that God's children are renewed in their waiting and strengthened for the battles ahead. The sanctuary is where God reveals His secrets to His children.

You are in the waiting room because the Lord is preparing you to carry an eternal weight of glory. Things birthed in the flesh usually come quickly but do not last, so wait with patience and perseverance, knowing that, *"our light affliction, which is but for a moment, worketh for us a far more exceeding and eternal weight of glory; While we look not at the things which are seen, but at the things which are not seen: for the things which are seen are temporal; but the things which are not seen are eternal"* (2 Corinthians 4:17-18).

CHAPTER 3
ISHMAEL-BIRTHED FROM THE FLESH

Spiritually speaking, the birthing of an Ishmael represents things we produce in the flesh because of an inability to wait on the promises of God. All of us at one time or another have produced something in the flesh, and have had to deal with the repercussions. Every born-again believer has multiple promises from God. Once we run ahead of God and get in our flesh, God has to come behind us and clean up the mess and set us on course for the fulfillment of His promises for our lives.

The Patriarch Abraham is considered the father of the faithful because the Bible states that he believed God and it was counted unto him for righteousness. Although the patriarch was a man of faith, he is credited along with his wife Sarah for conceiving and birthing the first Ishmael. The name Abraham means exalted father, but he was called Abram when the Lord first spoke to him. He was instructed to leave his family and that which was familiar in order to travel to a land the Lord would show him. The Lord promised him seven blessings, which meant God would complete and perfect a work in him. God promised to: *1) "Make a great nation out of him; 2) bless him. 3) make his name great; 4) make him a blessing; 5) bless those who blessed him; 6) curse those who cursed him; 7) bless all the families of the earth through him"* (Genesis 12:2-3).

Abram was seventy-five years old when he left Haran with his wife Sarai and his nephew Lot in pursuit of the promises of God. Sarai was sixty five at the time. You might feel like the years are passing you by with unfulfilled promises, but can you imagine being called by God in your seventies? When the Lord visited Abram and told him the He would be his shield and his exceeding great reward, his primary concern was the fact that he was childless because Sarai was barren. Having an heir to carry the family name was very important at that time and in that culture. Barrenness was considered a curse in the ancient world, and could be considered grounds for divorce. When Abram brought to God's attention the fact that he was childless and the heir in his house was not from his loins, God reassured him that his heir would most definitely be one birthed from his own body. That promise must have seemed strange to the patriarch since both he and his wife Sarai were well advanced in age. But God is not constrained by time because he operates independent of time. I love to describe God as the *God of 11:59* because if God promises that he will do something for you this year and you arrive at December 31st and the clock is showing 11:59 p.m., please don't panic because you serve the God who can suspend time if he has to in order to bring His promises to pass in your life. Don't dwell on the impossibility, or the improbability of your situation. Rejoice in the fact the His promises are yea and amen.

At some point between the promise of an heir and its fulfillment, while they are in the waiting room, Sarai convinces Abram to go with her maidservant Hagar. The Bible says that Abram heeded the voice of Sarai. Husbands should listen to their wives, but not when it involves something contrary to what is spoken by the Lord. A substitute wife when there was barrenness was a common practice of that time. The married woman who was unable to bear children was held in derision by her peers and was often required to give a female servant to her husband so an heir could be produced. Everything done out of tradition might not be of God so don't just follow tradition for it may lead to the birthing of something that is definitely not of God.

Many believers are stuck in a religious, traditional paradigm. Faith in what God has promised must always take precedent over the rudiments and traditions of men. We must learn to be patient in the waiting room. Genesis 15 records the promise God gave to Abram concerning an heir from his own body. Genesis 16 states that Abram had lived in the land of Canaan for ten years when Sarai gave him her maid Hagar to be his wife. Many years had passed since the promise so they decided to help God out. Time can appear as our enemy in the waiting room, depending on what we are waiting for, and the length of time we've been waiting. But God isn't going to do things prematurely simply because you are panicking in the waiting room. *"To every thing there is a season, and a time to every purpose under the heaven: A time to be born, and a time to die; a time to plant, and a time to pluck up that which is planted."* (Ecclesiastes 3:1-2). Like the old gospel song says, "He's an on-time God...He may not come when you want Him but He'll always be on time". So we might as well accept that fact and wait on the Lord.

Why didn't they concoct that plan for Abram to sleep with Hagar before the Lord promised him an heir? It is because the enemy always desires to bring a contrary word to us while we are in the waiting room. He wants us to birth something in the flesh that will interfere with our divine destiny. The Bible states, *"And Sarai Abram's wife took Hagar her maid the Egyptian, after Abram had dwelt ten years in the land of Canaan, and gave her to her husband Abram to be his wife. And he went in unto Hagar, and she conceived: and when she saw that she had conceived her mistress was despised in her eyes"* (Gen. 16:3)

The moment Hagar conceived she began to despise Sarai because she had given something to Abram that Sarai could not. Hagar might have felt superior to Sarai because she knew that an inability to conceive was frowned upon. Maybe she thought Abram would elevate her to the status of number one wife because she had given him the heir that Sarai could not. But Hagar represents works done in the flesh that masquerade as works of obedience. The son that she conceived brought confusion and strife into Abram's life, because things birthed prematurely and in the flesh cannot fulfill the promises of God. Under the Holy Spirits guidance, the Apostle Paul warns such works are symbolic of the old covenant: "*...[F]or it is written that Abraham had two sons: the one by a bondwoman, the other by a freewoman. But he who was of the bondwoman was born according to the flesh, and he of the freewoman through promise, which things are symbolic. For these are the two covenants: the one from Mount Sinai which gives birth to bondage, which is Hagar...[who] is in bondage with her children...Nevertheless what does the Scripture say? "Cast out the bondwoman and her son, for the son of the bondwoman shall not be heir with the son of the freewoman."* (Galatians 4:22—30). Flesh and spirit can't dwell in the same place. Faith and doubt are diametrically opposed to each other, where one is the other cannot operate. Light and darkness cannot co-exist together. So all such works of impatience, doubt, anxiety and human devising must be cast out, gotten rid of, if we are to receive the blessedness of God's promise for our lives.

God is merciful and long suffering and although Abram and Sarai went outside of God's will, He did not break His covenant with them. God is not going to cast you away because you birthed something in the flesh while in the waiting room. But the consequences of these "lapses of faith" often live on to our chagrin. The Lord visited Hagar and promised to multiply her seed exceedingly. He also told her that her son would be a wild man; his hand would be against every man, and every man's hand against him. You don't need to look any further than the events in the Middle East to see the fulfillment of that prophecy.

What's in a Name?

Abram was eighty-six years old when his son Ishmael was born. Thirteen years later when he had turned ninety-nine, the

Lord appeared before him and told him to walk before Him and be perfect. The Hebrew word for perfect is *tamiym (taw-meem');* and it means to have *integrity*, to be *complete*, to be *full*. It comes from a root which means *upright*, without *spot*, and *undefiled*. Although he and Sarai had stepped outside of His will, God returned to restore the covenant of faith with them and as a token of that renewal, changed his name to Abraham and changed her name to Sarah. God would make him the father of many nations and her, the mother of nations. Whenever God changed the names of certain people, it was to give them a new identity and to prepare them for another level of their walk in Him. The name change designated the difference between who they were and where they were to who they would become and where they would go. God changed Abraham's grandson's name from Jacob which means supplanter, to Israel which means having power with God. Jesus changed Simon's [God has heard] name to Peter [Rock]. Jacob had to wrestle with God and come away with a limp to get his name changed. On the other hand, God had to wrestle the trickster spirit out of Him before He could give him that name. It's going to cost us to get our names changed. The carnal nature does not die easily and must be killed daily. We will have to have to wrestle and limp and die to the flesh. But when God completes the birthing process in His people they will get their new name. *"...To him that overcometh will I give to eat of the hidden manna, and will give him a white stone, and in the stone a new name written, which no man knoweth saving he that receiveth it*" (Revelation 2:17). In order to eat of the hidden manna, receive the white stone, and receive the new name, we will have to turn away from, and give up the Ishmael's we've birthed in the waiting room, just like Abraham had to send away his son, Ishmael.

"And Abraham said unto God, O that Ishmael might live before thee!" (Gen 17:18). Abraham loved Ishmael and wanted him to live before God, but Ishmael was not the promised seed. I believe he wanted Ishmael to receive the blessing of the first born.

But God's word was adamant: *"Cast out the bondwoman and her son for he shall NOT inherit along with the son of promise."* There are Ishmael's in our lives that we love but God is not going to allow them to become part of the covenant, so we might as well walk away from them. It is not easy for us to part with people or things that we've grown accustomed to, but Isaac and Ishmael cannot dwell in the same house. If Isaac is to go forth then you must be willing to part with your Ishmael. As fore mentioned, many good Christian women have "birthed an Ishmael" by marrying a man out of their flesh. And like Abraham they plead for their Ishmaels to "live in His sight". They want God to bless marriages that are hopelessly out of His will and they themselves stay in these terrible marriages only because of the stigma of divorce and because they don't want to admit that their marriages were not ordained by God. They even develop a level of comfort in their very uncomfortable situation, because human beings learn to adapt to whatever environment they are in. It is like people losing their way in the woods. At first they feel lost and desperately try to find their way out. But after a while, they learn to survive in the woods. As time passes, they become accustomed to the woods. Finally, the woods become their home. Ultimately, when the rescue party shows up, they, who were once lost in the woods are now afraid to leave the woods because it has become their "home". They're scared of what awaits them outside of the same woods they once felt lost in. It actually saddens them to leave. There are individuals who have become so accustomed to being in prison that they commit crimes as soon as they are released. They function better behind bars than they do in society, and that is the reason the recidivism rate is so high. "O that Ishmael might live in your sight". That petition has ascended to God so many times as His children try to do in their humanity what God has promised to do in His divinity. But God does not need our help in order to fulfill His promises to us. He doesn't need that little bit of dishonesty or deception in order to get that permit for our church building. He doesn't need our manipulation of people in order to get them to give. He doesn't need us to embellish our testimony in order to make it more impacting. He doesn't need you to maneuver and show yourself up so that that man will notice you. No! No! No! God is God all by Himself and He and He alone will bring to pass that which he has promised. That is why He sometimes has to leave us a little longer in the waiting room—like he did with Abraham and Sarah— until we learn that crucial lesson. So when Sarah was as dried up as the Sinai wilderness, *"Sarah received strength to conceive seed, and was delivered of a child when she was past age."* (Hebrews 11:11). God, Himself had to intervene in Sarah's physiology, returning vitality to her womb, eggs to her ovaries and elasticity to her birth canal, in order for conception, gestation and delivery to take place so that she could birth the promised child.

When the Lord appeared to Abraham in the plains of Mamre and informed him that Sarah would bear a son, it seemed so impossible to Sarah, she laughed within herself and said, *"After I am waxed old shall I have pleasure, my lord being old also?"* (Gen 18:12). But that was just the point: God had to re-establish His sovereignty in their lives by doing that which would have been impossible without His intervention. It isn't about one's age or the deadness of one's womb or the impossibility of one's situation. It is about the creative power of the Eternal God who *"spoke and it was done, [who] commanded and it stood fast"* (Psalms 33:9). Be careful not to scoff or laugh within yourself at the prospect of God taking a situation that appears to be dead in your life and breathing life into it because you will be tempted to try to do things your own way, or worse yet, to give in to despair and give up on God, laughing skeptically like Sarah did, "Can God really do anything for me?" The Lord's response to that question is the same one he asked Abraham, *"Is anything too hard for the Lord?"* (Genesis 18:14). At the set time spoken by God, Sarah received a visitation from the Lord and bore a son, whose very name, Isaac [*laughter*], would not only be a reminder to Sarah of her doubt, but greater still, would be a testimony to all that God can turn the laughter of skepticism and despair into animated laughter of joy.

It is significant that God reiterates the promises made to Abraham to Isaac. He promises 1) to be with him 2) to bless him. 3) to give Isaac and his seed the surrounding countries 4) to perform the oath He swore to Abraham 5) to multiply Isaac's seed as the stars of the heaven 6) God reaffirms His promise concerning the surrounding countries. 7) to bless all the nations of the earth in Isaac's seed. It is because the tendency to revert to old patterns of behavior—even after having birthed the promise—is very real and often asserts itself in a crisis. For Isaac to prosper in his covenanted position, he must continue the tradition of faith established by Abraham. He could not afford to forget the testing of Abraham's faith. Even after the birth of the promise, faith never ceases to be the key to unlock heaven's storehouse and release the protection and continued blessing of God over the "Isaacs" of our lives. That is why during his sojourning in Gerar, during a time of famine, the Lord appeared unto him and told him not to go down to Egypt but to dwell in the land of Gerar (Genesis 26:1—5). In spite of the circumstances, he must exercise faith that God would provide for him, so the promise given to Abraham would not fail. The birth of the promise does not mean the end of faith and dependence on the Lord. In fact, it calls for just as much and even greater faith to nurture and preserve the blessedness of the promise. There are persons who forget that their prosperity and success came from God and they begin to boast and live in the flesh and become selfish and arrogant. They treat the blessing as irreversible, as securely theirs, but God may send a famine to remind them that all that they possess is the Lord's and came from Him.

The Life of Faith Versus Life In The Flesh

To continue to enjoy the promise, one must continue to live the life of faith. When the Lord formed man from the dust of the ground, he breathed into man's nostrils and man became a living soul or *nephesh* [Hebrew: usually representative of the animalistic functions and appetites of the body]. In other words, your physical body represents all that you are. And the most powerful drives in a human being are those drives that seek to preserve one's life: food, shelter, sex. That makes sense, for if the body dies, the very expression of our existence ceases. In a similar fashion, if the body is malnourished or is sickly and deficient, our spirit man will be negatively affected and our ability to worship and serve God will be diminished. That is why "soul" came to be considered the seat or center of a person's intellect, will, and emotions, for the very expressions of who we are, our thoughts, decisions, desires and feelings—be these of a spiritual or carnal nature— manifest themselves through our physical being. The "soul" therefore can either be controlled by the flesh—those physical, existential drives that often lead to carnality [Greek: *sarx*, here referring to our fallen human nature with its frailties and lustful passion]—or by the Spirit of God. If lead by the flesh the "soul" will then become a womb of carnality, birthing selfishness, sensuousness and works of death. That explains why Paul wrote to the Romans: *"For I know that in me (that is, in my flesh, [*my sarx*]) dwelleth no good thing: for to will is present with me; but how to perform that which is good I find not" (Rom 7:18).* But if controlled by the Spirit, the soul will bring forth works of love and true obedience.

We cannot deny that fleshly appetites are sweet to the taste; if they were not then we would not keep going back to them time and time again. It is like the fast foods we love that are slowly killing us. (Never mind that double cheeseburger and diet cola sitting next to you as you read this) We know that we should avoid them and should be eating salad instead, but they taste so good, we go back for more. The same could be said of illicit sex, or anger, or any of the many works of the flesh. The danger is that we sometimes want to serve God and do His will while operating in the flesh, thinking that these tainted works will be pleasing to God. But the prophet Isaiah warns us that *"we are all like an unclean thing, and all our righteousness*—legalistic or humanistic works of obedience— *are like filthy rags."* (Isaiah 64:6) We cannot birth anything good from the flesh. That was exactly what Jeremiah tried to convey to his legalistic brethren in Jerusalem: *"Can the Ethiopian change his skin or the leopard its spots? Then may you also do good, that are accustomed to do evil."* (Jeremiah 13:23) We cannot allow the devil to deceive us into thinking there is anything redeemable in the flesh. The flesh must die, Ishmael must go. In *Galatians 5:17* Paul talks about the works of the flesh that are manifest, which means they are clearly seen. Some of them are *adultery, fornication, witchcraft, hatred, murders*. Works birthed out from these tainted fountains may masquerade as works of obedience and righteousness but they only bring forth death and God's disapproval. In the Day of Judgment many preachers and miracle workers, men and women who healed the sick, cast out demons, prophesied in Christ's name and did many other wonders, will receive the shock of their lives when Christ denounces them as "workers of iniquity". (See Matthew 7:21—23) May we all have our eyes opened to discern, and be delivered from, works of the flesh, especially those that masquerade as works of righteousness and obedience. Unlike Abraham who pleaded, *"O that Ishmael might live before thee!"* (Genesis 17:18), let us "*Cast out the bondwoman and her child" (*Genesis 21:10).

God is not looking for perfect people; He is looking for people to perfect. We must allow the Lord to take us to a place where there is no room in us for the enemy to get a foothold. The devil's operating theatre is the flesh, so it must be crucified. We must die daily because the carnal nature is always trying to creep up on us. According to Paul, we must not conform to this world's system, but be transformed by the renewing of our minds. Our carnal minds are like an old dilapidated building that must be renovated. Every ungodly thought must be torn down and replaced by thoughts of things that are pure and Godly. This is not an easy process because as foresaid, the mind is more prone to the carnal and worldly. The strongholds that have been erected for many years in our minds will not be torn down overnight. Some of these strongholds are well fortified areas where spirits— spirits of perversion and lust, spirits of drug addiction, spirits of homosexuality and lesbianism, just to name a few— are well entrenched and they must be driven out. We must make an honest assessment of ourselves (I Corinthians 11:28) and not pretend that these strongholds do not exist. That is what the waiting room is for: the opportunity to be cleansed and freed from all that defiles. If not, the enemy will wait until our promotion and elevation to expose these areas of our lives. In this way, he will not only affect us but others also. We must constantly guard against complacency while in the waiting room. Every waking moment must be spent asking the Holy Spirit to search us in order to determine what is in us that is not pleasing to Him.

CHAPTER 4
WALK BY FAITH AND NOT BY SIGHT:

The King the Killing and the Calf.

The Bible gives many examples of people who did things out of their flesh while waiting. The Bible's openness about the weaknesses of the men and women used by God is one of the awesome things about it. It does not gloss over or cover up the character flaws in the lives of God's heroes. That is why, as believers, we can identify with them because they were not supermen and superwomen; they were regular people used by God to do His work. John 1:6 says, *"There was a man sent from God."* It does not say a "superman". James 5:17 says, *"Elias was a man subject to like passions as we are."*

On Asking for a King

When you contrast the life of David with the life of Saul, it is evident that David was a man after God's heart and Saul was a man after the people's heart. David made his share of mistakes in the waiting room, but unlike Saul he was truly repentant. David's primary interest was pleasing God, but Saul always seemed to care more about pleasing his flesh. He looked to the people for his deliverance and not to God. His life epitomizes the life of an individual who puts his trust in numbers instead of the Lord.

The Lord raised up Samuel to be a prophet-priest and judge to the nation of Israel because Eli's priesthood had been rejected due to his negligence in training his sons, Hophni and Phinehas, to be true men of God. They, themselves, turned out to be wicked, profane men who disqualified themselves from being used by God as leaders of Israel. The demise of Eli's and his sons' priesthood/leadership opened the door for the Prophet Samuel to lead the nation. When Samuel was old he appointed his sons Joel and Abiah to be judges. But unfortunately, like Hophni and Phinehas, Samuel's sons were corrupt. They refused to walk in the way of their father who was an anointed man of God. So the people asked Samuel for a king so that they might be rid of the excesses of his sons. They also wanted to like the surrounding nations. But this request, while seemingly justified because Samuel was old and his sons were corrupt, was really a rejection of God's rule over them (See I Samuel 8:7). God never intended for His people to be like other nations; He raised them up to be a model and a paradigm for the nations, to lead them from their heathen practices so they might follow the true God.

Samuel was so displeased by the people's request that he took it to the Lord in prayer. The Lord told him to honor their request and He also warned them about the dire consequences of having a king. But the people refused to listen. Saul was chosen to be king, but 1 Samuel 10:21b-23 gives us an early glimpse of his leadership skills: *"And when they sought for him, he could not be found. Therefore they inquired of the Lord further, if the man should yet come thither. And the Lord answered, Behold, he hath hid himself among the stuff."* Saul's presentation before the people as king should have been the beginning of the greatest time of his life, but what do we see? He is hiding among the stuff, the military baggage. From the outset he displays a lack of leadership that would dog him throughout the course of his reign. Saul's kingship began because the people rejected God. It is difficult to get something good out of a rejection of God. He was never able to earn the respect of the people. The people had to run and fetch him out of hiding. When he came forth he had the outer appearance of a strong leader because he was taller than all the people. Unfortunately outward appearance does not guarantee great leadership.

Obedience Rather Than Sacrifice: God's Delays Are Not Denials

There are two incidents in the life of Saul that show his lack of inner strength and represent turning points in his life and leadership. Samuel had told him: *"And thou shalt go down before me to Gilgal; and, behold I will come down unto thee, to offer burnt offerings, and to sacrifice sacrifices of peace offerings: seven days shalt thou tarry, till I come to thee, and show thee what thou shalt do"* (1 Samuel 10:8). In this first incident, he panics in the waiting room by making a sacrifice when *"...he waited seven days, according to the time set by Samuel. But Samuel did not come to Gilgal; and the people were scattered from him. So Saul said, "Bring me a burnt offering and peace offerings here to me."* (I Samuel 13:8, 9). Offering the sacrifice was Samuel's prerogative, not Saul's and he usurped authority and position when he did. But why did he do it? Because he was too proud to admit he was afraid, and too full of doubt to exercise faith. The Philistines had gathered themselves together *"to fight with Israel, thirty thousand chariots and six thousand horsemen, and people as the sand which is on the seashore in multitude"* (Verse 5) at Michmash. The people, terrified, ran away from him and hid in caves, thickets, rocks, high places, and pits because they were hopelessly outnumbered and outmatched. This was an opportunity for the king to show strong leadership by rallying the people and instilling confidence in them. Instead, he superstitiously decided to offer the sacrifice and not wait any longer for Samuel. "*When I saw that the people were scattered from me, and that you did not come within the days appointed, and that the Philistines gathered together at Michmash, then I said, 'The Philistines will now come down on me at Gilgal, and* ***I have not made supplication to the Lord.' I forced myself*** *therefore, and offered a burnt offering."* (I Samuel 13:11, 12). Somehow, he must have thought, if I do the sacrifice, it will not only give the people back their courage, but it may give us the victory over the Philistines. Such acts of desperation offered as acts of devotion and faith may placate our troubled minds but they are offensive to God. Notice how he implies that he had no other choice but to offer the sacrifice. "I forced myself", he says. No wonder Samuel told him that he had done foolishly. Even though his sacrifice was an act of religious service, it was not counted as righteousness but disobedience.... *"You have not kept the commandment of the Lord."* (I Samuel 13: 13). Saul pushed the panic button because of his lack of faith and inner strength. He excused his disobedience because of his lack of humility and contrition. How about you, my dear brother, my sister? Are you masking your doubt with zeal, your disobedience with religion?

Saul's actions in this incident are so reminiscent of many believers who appropriate to themselves prerogatives that belong to others. They display great zeal for the things of God, but their motives and modus operandi are contrary to God's way. They politic on church boards; utter innuendos about other's characters; encroach on other's ministries, all for the cause, they say, but they are really motivated by a spirit of fault finding, jealousy and selfishness.

There are also great lessons for leaders in this incident with Saul. In ministry, there will come turbulent times when the people will become restless and their confidence in the ministry will wane and they may start to move away when things don't quite work out as planned. The first great lesson is that leaders must never panic in the waiting room when the people become restless because there are Godly delays. Leaders must continue to trust

God in Gilgal and realize that victory comes from the Lord of Hosts and not from the number of the people. God is famous for doing more with less, as he did in the time of Gideon. God is not pleased when we put our trust in numbers because it shows a lack of confidence in God and it robs Him of His glory in the victory.

The second great lesson involves Saul's plan of action to deal with the situation. He becomes restless because the people are in disarray. But instead of fasting, praying, and seeking the face of the Lord in order to renew his strength and receive divine wisdom, he decides to take on the role of the priest. The road becomes very dangerous when an individual does not "remain in his lane". Samuel was the one to offer the sacrifice, not Saul. King Uzziah did the same thing and was struck with leprosy when he decided to usurp the authority of the priest and burn incense in the temple.

There are too many people in the ministry operating outside of their lane with disastrous results. The five-fold ministry must operate in unity and not try to work contrary to each other. We don't need the choir director trying to pastor the church; if you have an anointing to lead the choir, then lead the choir and leave the running of the church to the pastor and the leadership team he has assigned. Perhaps you can preach a good message. Perhaps you have. It does not mean that you can run a church. The man or woman of God might have their short comings but the anointing for leading the church is on them not on you. Deacons need to stay in their lanes and not try to manipulate the pastor with their purse strings. God is not pleased and the work is hampered when this spirit of usurpation exists in the church. We must kill the spirit of Absalom, and the rebellion of Korah in the church.

The third great lesson is that leaders must accept responsibility for their actions and not blame others or circumstances for their lapses. Saul's insinuation that he had no choice but to offer the sacrifice because of Samuel's delay and the people's fear, amounts to his blaming Samuel, the people, and even the Philistines for his disobedience. But Samuel looked beyond the excuses and zeroed in on the real issue and told Saul, *"thou has not kept the commandment of the Lord thy God."* (1 Sam. 13:13). Obedience is not optional, nor is it negotiable depending on the circumstances. It is the requirement expected of every believer, and especially of leaders.

The fourth great lesson is this: Do not come out of the waiting room prematurely because the time of your promotion might be imminent and you will miss it if you move hastily. What is the purpose of waiting so long then missing the breakthrough when it is right at your fingertips? God speaks to us in the waiting room and gives us instructions and we must be obedient. If anxiety and doubt cause you to move ahead of God, or to compromise yourself, and an Ishmael is birthed, please don't play the blame game. Don't blame God, or your circumstances, or the people you thought would have done this or that who didn't. Just take responsibility for what you have done. Repent quickly and ask the Lord to forgive your transgression. God is a merciful God and repentance is the first step to receiving His mercy and reviving the promise.

The second incident involved Saul's sparing the life of Agag, king of the Amalekites when Samuel had told him, quite categorically, to *"go and attack Amalek, and utterly destroy all that they have, and do not spare them. But kill man and woman, infant and nursing child, ox and sheep, camel and donkey."* (I Samuel 15: 3). Amalek had launched an attack against Israel when they had left Egypt and God told Moses to write down what they had done as a memorial of their dastardly act because He would blot out the remembrance of Amalek from under heaven. (See Exodus 17:8—14.) Saul was to be the instrument of retribution to Amalek and he was instructed to kill everyone and everything. Besides, the Amalekites were a band of idolatrous guerilla terrorists, and God knew His people would never be able to live peacefully in the Promised Land as long as the Amalekites existed. Saul attacked and defeated the Amalekites but he did not utterly destroy them. He spared King Agag and the best of the sheep, oxen, and the fatlings of the lamb. The word of the Lord came to Samuel that God had rejected Saul from being king over Israel. Samuel was grieved and cried unto the Lord all night. (We can't afford to cry and mourn for those whom God rejects for continually birthing Ishmaels of disobedience).

When Samuel came to Saul, Saul told him that he had carried out the Lord's commandment. Mission Accomplished. Samuel's response was, *"What meaneth then this bleating of the sheep in mine ears, and the lowing of the oxen which I hear?"* (1 Sam. 15:14). And why is King Agag still alive? Just as he had done at Michmash, Saul decided to play the blame game by claiming that *"they [the people] have brought them from the Amalekites: for the people spared the best of the sheep and of the oxen, to sacrifice unto the Lord thy God; and the rest we have utterly destroyed."* (I Samuel 15:20) How pathetic. He was the leader and he had received the instructions from God on how to deal with the Amalekites. So it was HIS responsibility to make sure that those instructions were carried out. Sparing the livestock to offer sacrifice to God did not negate the command given. God does not want a polluted sacrifice, birthed out of rebellion and disobedience. God doesn't need anyone to rob a bank, play the lottery or sell drugs to give tithes and offerings. Saul insists that he had done what the Lord required: *"Yea, I have obeyed the voice of the LORD, and have gone the way which the LORD sent me, and have brought Agag the king of Amalek, and have utterly destroyed the Amalekites. But the people took of the spoil, sheep and oxen, the chief of the things which should have been utterly destroyed, to sacrifice unto the LORD thy God in Gilgal"* (1 Samuel 15:21) In other words, it wasn't him, but the people who made the decision. Some leader! He tries to throw the people under the bus in an attempt to save his own skin, but the prophet would have none of it. He rebukes him and tells him that the Lord's delight is not in burnt offerings and sacrifices but in obedience to the voice of the Lord. He compares Saul's rebellion and stubbornness to witchcraft, iniquity and idolatry (See I Samuel 15:22, 23). Many people are on the altar offering polluted sacrifices to the Lord from an unrepentant heart. A sacrifice from a heart that is not right is nothing but vain religion.

Saul finally comes clean. He tells the prophet that he sinned because he feared the people and obeyed their voice. When a leader continually allows the people to lead him contrary to the voice of God he will eventually lose his ability to lead those people because they will lose all respect for him. But more than that, he will also lose God's respect and anointing. This is the reason why there was never any true allegiance for Saul by the people. His confession could not save his kingdom because he had proved himself unfit. Notice that God gave Saul a second chance to prove himself. Notice that where Saul failed in this situation is the same area in which he failed at Michmash: an inability to stand firm on the word of God, obeying it implicitly and not to blame either circumstance or person for his decisions and actions. In other words, Saul was "recycled" through the waiting room to see if he would learn the lessons of true leadership. And so it is with us as well. We are made to face the same challenges and difficulties that defeat us, time and time again, until we defeat them. As long as we don't learn the lessons, we will face the challenge until we do, or are finally rejected.

Saul never recovered from his fear of the people; he never came to the realization that the Lord was his strength and not the people. He begged Samuel to go worship with him as a public demonstration before the people that he had Samuel's support. If the prophet did not go to worship with the king the people would realize that God's hand was no longer with the king. This would cause the people to lose all confidence in the king. Samuel's response to Saul paints a tragic picture of his downward spiral. Samuel said, *"I will not return with thee: for thou has rejected the word of the Lord, and the Lord hath rejected thee from being king over Israel"* (1 Sam. 15:26). Saul continued to beg and Samuel finally acquiesced. After the worship Samuel went to Ramah, and Saul went up to his house in Gibeah. The next time we hear about Saul he is being tormented by an evil spirit, and has to be soothed by the music of a young David; the man after God's heart who would replace him as king.

Saul's life was never marked by true repentance. From the time he birthed the first Ishmael in the waiting room while waiting for the Prophet Samuel, his life took a downward spiral that eventually lead him to consult a woman that had a familiar spirit, and finally, in despair, to commit suicide. That desperate act was done after he was severely wounded by the Philistine archers and begged his armor bearer to take his life. He died by his own hands when, after his armor bearer refused to strike him, he fell on his sword, a victim of the *Ishmael* of doubt, fear, disobedience, pride, and blame casting, that he had birthed in the waiting room at Michmash and nurtured in the palace at Gibeah. Saul faced death the same way he faced life, by taking matters into his own hands and by his refusal to trust God. His life is an example to every leader of how imperative it is for them to trust the voice of the Lord and not to lean on their own understanding.

Obedience And Temptation From Within: Why Idleness Is Dangerous

David was God's choice to replace Saul. He is called the sweet psalmist of Israel and a man after God's own heart, but he birthed an Ishmael during a time of idleness when, instead of being out on the battle field with his men, he tarried at Jerusalem. Tarrying is not a problem when you are instructed by the Lord to tarry, as was the case when the believers tarried at Jerusalem for the indwelling of the Holy Spirit. When we tarry because of an idle mind, that mind becomes the playground of the devil, and all manner of evil and concupiscence—sexual desire, lust—can be birthed. Once the mind is idle it begins to think on things that are pleasing to the flesh.

It was the time when kings went out to battle. But for whatever reason, David decided to stay at "home". His success as a warrior and king had made him indolent. Instead of running from Saul, living in the wilderness and in caves; instead of having to deal with the disrespect of a Nabal, he was now king over all Israel. Long gone were the days of dwelling in the cave of Adullam, taking care of many broke and distressed people; long gone were the days of having to send his young men to ask foolish Nabal for provision. Now he was living in the palace, enjoying the trappings of the life of ease. God's leaders should never become idle and derelict in their duties, especially after they have reached the "third level of the anointing" and have birthed the vision. When their ministries have been birthed and are thriving, they must resist the tendency to become lazy and to begin to stray. Instead, they must remember always the time spent in the waiting room when they fasted, prayed and sacrificed a great deal of time and finances in order to bring their ministry from the fetal stage to the birthing. And they must strive to maintain that spirit of diligence, humility, faith and integrity. Reader, you're not living in the cramped apartment anymore. You're in the big house now. Your finances have increased. The cars are in the driveway. You have the husband you've always dreamed of, the wife you've always wanted. Your ministry is exploding and success accompanies your every move. In short, life is good; God has blessed. Be careful. Don't take your blessedness for granted. Don't start losing your grip on God or dependence on His word. Avoid the spirit of "sit back and relax". Beware of idleness.

That is what happened to David and set the stage for him committing perhaps the worst sin of his life. While tarrying at the palace at Jerusalem, he took an evening stroll upon the roof of his house and saw Bathsheba washing herself. When he saw her beautiful nakedness, his mind was impregnated with thoughts of having her. He was so consumed by her beauty that he never thought to turn away, unlike Job who had *"... made a covenant with mine eyes; why then should I think upon a maid?"* (Job31:1). The Bible talks about the three areas in which a man will be enticed into temptation: the lust of the flesh, the lust of the eyes and the pride of life. It first begins with our looking at the desired thing, then our flesh is stimulated, then our pride convinces us that we must have it. And that is exactly what happened to David. He sent for Bathsheba and slept with her.

The Apostle James said, *"But every man is tempted, when he is drawn away of his own lust, and enticed. Then when lust hath conceived, it bringeth forth sin: and sin, when it is finished, bringeth forth death"* (James 1:14-15). David's lust had brought forth sin, and with it, its consequences: Bathsheba had become pregnant. Sin had begun to pay its wages: death (see Romans 6:23). Bathsheba was Uriah's wife, and David had committed a trespass when he slept with her. Her "unplanned pregnancy" was definitely not in either David's or Bathsheba's plans, so she sent—I am sure with a certain degree of trepidation—to tell David about this turn of events. Sleeping with her was bad enough, but her pregnancy put David in a very tight spot indeed. To cover up the pregnancy, David sent for Uriah from the battlefield hoping he would sleep with his wife so the baby to be born would be considered his. But Uriah, faithful soldier that he was, refused to go home to his wife but slept outside the palace. Desperate, David concocted the scheme to have Uriah killed by having Uriah placed in the heat of the battle and then having the men retreat and leave him unsupported. God reprimanded David through the prophet Nathan who also let David know that the child born to Bathsheba would die. In spite of David's entreaties to the Lord, the baby still died. David was the leader of his people. It was his responsibility to uphold the law. If God had spared the child's life, it would have somehow insinuated that God had overlooked his sin and he had gotten away with it. This would have unleashed a spirit of presumption that would have lead to unbridled sinfulness in Israel.

Besides, God had to divorce himself from David's sin which gave the Lord's enemies great occasion to blaspheme.

The Nathans Of Our Lives

Psalm 51 is the beautiful psalm of repentance David wrote to express his heartfelt sorrow for having sinned against the Lord when he slept with Bathsheba and had Uriah killed. His cry to God in verse 10 should be the cry of sinner and saint alike: *"Create in me a clean heart, O God; and renew a right spirit within me"* (Psalm 51:10). What a difference between David and Saul. Saul's excuses paint a pathetic picture of un-repentance while David's repentance proves that a broken and a contrite heart the Lord will not despise. Unlike Saul, David understood that God's true sacrifice is not a burnt animal but a broken and contrite heart.

There is also a stark contrast between how David and Saul responded to the births of their respective Ishmael's. Saul always blamed someone else, sought to cover up his disobedience with religious acts, and never exhibited true repentance or accountability. David, on the other hand, behaved differently. When the Prophet Nathan confronted David with the words "*thou art the man.*"(II Samuel 12:7), referring to his sin with Bathsheba and his murder of Uriah, his immediate response was, *"I have sinned against the LORD."* (II Samuel 12:13). There was immediate accountability on the part of David, and because of that the Lord forgave him and spared his life. If you have birthed an Ishmael in the waiting room and are suffering from the depression of your loss of the Lord's presence and favor, accept Isaiah's counsel and *"Seek the Lord while He may be found; call upon Him while He is near. Let the wicked forsake his way and the unrighteous man his thoughts and return unto the Lord; and He will have mercy and abundantly pardon."* (Isaiah 55: 6, 7). Come and receive the refreshing of the Lord.

Abraham wanted Ishmael to live before God, Samuel cried all

night before the Lord for Saul; David fasted and prostrated himself on the ground as he sought the Lord for the child. Once the child died David got up from the ground, washed himself and worshiped the Lord. Once we come to the realization that the thing we are fasting and crying out to the Lord for is dead; we must get up from the ground, wash ourselves and continue to worship the Lord. Too many people are continuing to fast and cry over dead things. If the relationship is dead, don't continue to lay down in sack cloth and ashes. Be like David, get up and worship! Be like Samuel, start looking for the person after God's heart.

Every believer should have a Nathan in his or her life. We must have Nathans who are bold enough to confront us when we birth something from the flesh because, according to the word of God, "a true witness delivers souls." When our Nathans expose our Ishmaels, we must not be arrogant and un-repentant like Saul. To do so would be to jeopardize our calling with the Lord and place us outside of the reach of God's grace. The Lord doesn't want us to cover up our sins with excuses. He confronts us with our sins, our Ishmaels, not to destroy us but to bring us back on course, to release us from the prisons of guilt and ineffectiveness that they place us in. Pride will cause us to reject the correction of our Nathans, but better to have our flesh hurting for a season than to miss what God has for us. Proverbs 27:6 says, *"faithful are the wounds of a friend: but the kisses of an enemy are deceitful."*

Unbelief And Rebellion: The Golden Calf

> *"And when the people saw that Moses delayed to come down out of the mount, the people gathered themselves together unto Aaron, and said unto him, Up, make us gods, which shall go before us; for as for this Moses, the man that brought us up out of the land of Egypt, we wot not what is become of him"* (Exodus 32:1).

Of all the men on the face of the earth, there is no one the Bible describes as being as meek as the man Moses. I imagine he needed that level of meekness in order to lead a church of over 1 million ex-slaves out of Egypt and through the wilderness. I believe this meekness was developed over time in the waiting room because when we first meet Moses as an adult, he kills an Egyptian for hitting one of the Hebrews. His leadership skills and patience were constantly tested because he led a people described by God as stiff-necked and rebellious. If some leaders today feel like the members are wearing them out, imagine what Moses went through. You have a congregation of thirty and you're feeling the effects of the lack of commitment, of the murmuring and complaining, multiply that by a million and you'll know what Moses experienced.

The Israelites knew the might and power of God because they had seen what he did to Pharaoh when he refused to let them go. Now they were at the base of the mount trembling because of the awe of God's presence. God had promised Abraham that He would make a great nation out of his descendants, and now He was about to give them the Law in order to prepare them to be who He had called them to be. Exodus 19 and 20 record the meeting at Mount Sinai, the giving of the law, the display of God's glory and the people's awe at being in His presence. But by the time we get to Exodus 32, the people are rebelling because they feel Moses has delayed in coming down from the mount. Moses had spent 40 days in the mount with God where he received the law, written with God's own finger on two tables of stone. What arrogance and lack of patience. The irony however is that they began to rebel at the very time Moses is preparing to come down from the mount. (But Israel was never very good at waiting on the Lord in any case. They constantly whined, murmured, and complained throughout their journey. In fact their whole history is littered with their unmitigated lack of patience and confidence in the Divine plan for them.) Very many times people give in and give up just at the point of their breakthrough. Are you about to give up right at the time when God is about to do something great in you? Are you about to move when you should be standing firmly on the Word of God?

God's delays are not denials. Moses had gone up the mountain to receive instructions from God in order to lead the people to the Promised Land. Moses could not come out of the presence of the Lord before he was released by God. He could not be released until he had received all the instructions that God had for him. (Neither can we be released from the waiting room until we have received all that the Lord has to teach us.) Let's examine a few of the people's complaints: Exodus 15: 2-26: they complain about a lack of water; Exodus 16: 2-3: they complain about a lack of food; Exodus 17:1-3: they complain again about a lack of water; Exodus 32:1: they complain about Moses' absence, this time going as far as asking for gods to lead them back to Egypt. Israel never seemed to get the picture: God is testing you to see if you will walk in His laws or not, refining you to truly make you a light to the Gentiles (see Deuteronomy 8:2-6; 4:5, 6). When the people said to Moses, *"Would to God we had died by the hand of the Lord in the land of Egypt, when we sat by the flesh pots, and when we did eat bread to the full; for ye have brought us forth into this wilderness, to kill this whole assembly with hunger"* (Exodus 16:3), they were in fact denying their miraculous deliverance from Egypt and professing that God was not able to sustain them. There was a constant atmosphere of complaining and lack of trust in God that permeated Israel's experience. Worse yet, they insulted God by claiming that Egypt was a better provider for them. For instance, God had parted the Red Sea for them, provided meat and bread for them but yet they had the gall to ask whether God was with them or not? (Verse 17). For the Israelites to even ask that question speaks of a deliberate unwillingness to believe and trust. It points to the nurturing of a spirit of ingratitude that refuses to accept the blessings received as true blessings but to look at them as minor things in the great scheme of things, to minimize the importance of the blessings received while magnifying the frustrations of those things not yet received. That is why their command to Aaron to make them gods was so egregious, and almost cost them their place in God's eternal plan. Believers today need to beware of developing that same spirit of wicked unbelief and ingratitude. We need to understand that when we don't get the things we hope and pray for, when we hope and pray for them, it doesn't mean that God has abandoned us, but simply that He is working out the counsels of His own will and wisdom and expects us to trust Him where we can't trace Him. While we're waiting, let us keep in mind that the worst Ishmaels that can be birthed are those of ingratitude and *wicked unbelief.* So if, while in the waiting room you are enticed to erect a golden idol because the prophetic word for your life does not appear to be coming to pass, remember your God of the last breakthrough and stand firm against the enemy's attempt to get you to birth something in the flesh. Your wait might appear to be long, but if you birth something in the flesh you will have to deal with the consequences, so again, I say to you, wait on the Lord and be of good courage.

Obedience Against All Odds: Moses' Great Sin

Once again the people began to murmur, singing the same old song, wondering why Moses had guided them into the wilderness to die, and wishing they had died with their brethren. The crisis? They had no water. But this was nothing new. Time and again God had come through for them. They had seen His wondrous works and Moses had been a faithful and patient leader. But this new round of griping got to Moses in a way that caused him to do that which he never had before: disobey a direct command of God. Moses was instructed to speak to the rock before the congregation, and the rock would bring forth water for the people and their livestock. But Moses is so disgusted with the people by this time, gathering the congregation before the rock, he reproaches them, *"Hear now, ye rebels; must we fetch you water out of this rock?"* (Numbers 20:10). You can hear the pent up frustration of this leader who has put up with the constant murmuring and complaining of this rebellious people for so long. And with those words, he strikes the rock twice, a deliberate act of rebellion. Because of this act of disobedience, both he and Aaron will be denied entrance to the Promised Land. Like Moses, there are many leaders who are at the breaking point because they are dealing with a flock that refuses to get with the vision. These men and women of God are totally frustrated. But the word of God to you is, don't break. Obey the word and speak to The Rock. Speak to Jesus and ask Him to pour out the water of the Holy Spirit on your parched, tired soul.

How tragic that Moses should have allowed the people to push him to the brink. *"They angered him also at the waters of strife, so that it went ill with Moses for their sakes: Because they provoked his spirit, so that he spake unadvisedly with his lips."* (Psalm 106: 32, 33) After 40 years of faithful service, Moses finds himself on the receiving end of God's justice; 40 years leading a people that chided with him every step of the way only to miss his opportunity to enter in. So close and yet so far! Church folk will wear you out and cause you to miss what God has for you if you allow them to. Moses not only allowed the people to anger him but to vex his spirit, causing him to disobey God. (Pastor, leader, shepherd, they are doing what they are doing because they want to vex your spirit and cause you to birth an Ishmael instead of bringing forth the promise). His punishment may seem harsh for an act that seems so trifling and for someone who had endured constant nagging and complaining from an ungrateful people. However, the Ishmaels birthed by a leader are a more serious affair because, as a leader, what he does has a potent effect on the people following him. Please be not deceived, leaders will be judged and held to a higher standard because of the influence they have on people. And although Moses' action might seem small and inconsequential, it wasn't. It was actually birthed from impatience, anger, frustration and presumption. Besides, he robbed God of His glory and tarnished the message of hope and love the miracle was supposed to convey. He also inadvertently "confirmed" what the people had been saying all along, that it was Moses who was leading them and not God. The ultimate irony is, like those that murmured, Miriam, Aaron, and Moses died short of the promise land. This is a solemn warning to every leader. You may have had many years of faithful ministry but then allow resentment or anger to cause you to act foolishly and disqualify you from further effectiveness. Humility, prayer, a forgiving spirit and strict obedience are the only safeguards against a leader birthing an Ishmael of frustrated disobedience.

CHAPTER 5
CONCEPTION

"*And Adam knew Eve his wife; and she conceived, and bare Cain, and said, I have gotten a man from the LORD*" (Gen. 4:1) Conception, the fertilization and formation of the zygote from the union of sperm and egg, This is the first stage of the birthing process. And it is one of the most extraordinary events that can be experienced. In spite of the fact that the proponents of abortion try to make people believe that the life of the baby does not begin at conception, that is a fallacy. The Lord told Jeremiah that He knew him before He formed him in his mother's womb. (Jeremiah 1:5). Jeremiah also wrote, "*Because he slew me not from the womb; or that my mother might have been my grave, and her womb to be always great with me*" (Jeremiah 20:17). He acknowledges that even as a zygote in his mother's womb, God saw him as a living entity and had a plan for his life.

Even science recognizes this reality, albeit for different reasons and from a different perspective. For instance, there are key things that can be determined about the baby as early as the time of fertilization. The sex of the baby can be determined at fertilization. In her book, *Introduction to Maternity & Pediatric Nursing,* Gloria Leifer writes, "*Developmental milestones exist in fetal growth and development as they do in growth and development after birth. Three basic stages characterize prenatal development: the zygote, the embryo, and the fetus. The second to the eighth week of development is known as the embryonic stage, with the developing infant called an embryo. From the ninth week of development until birth the developing infant is called a fetus. By the tenth week the external genitalia are visible to ultrasound examination. By the second week after fertilization the ectoderm, endoderm, and amnion begin to develop. By the third week the mesoderm and neural tube form and the primitive heart begins to pump."* (Leifer chapter 3 page 37). Life is truly a mystery of which conception is the initial stage.

Conception takes place when the man and woman come together in intimate contact through sex. In God's original plan, this sexual encounter should have been the expression of deep love and bonding, although that seldom happens in the world today. The man deposits his sperm into the woman who becomes not only a receptacle, but also the nurturer, protector and developer of this new life. In Scripture, this act of intimacy, leading to conception, is fittingly called "knowing". So the Scripture describes the first couple's sexual encounter in the following manner: *"And Adam **knew** Eve his wife and she conceived...."* (Genesis 4:1). When the angel Gabriel came to Mary to inform her that she would have a son, Mary responded by saying, *"how shall this be, seeing I know not a man?"* (Luke 1:34). Likewise, the Lord wants to know His people in the manner that Adam knew his wife Eve. This knowing speaks of intimacy that produces conception. He has not created us to be mediocre or average. He would not have given Heaven's best for our redemption if he had not planned on birthing something great out of us. The price He paid for our salvation is proof that we are valuable to him. He desires to take us into the secret place through intimate worship, and in that sacred moment impregnate our spirit with a word. That word is a seed He plants in us, akin to the planting of a zygote—the union of sperm and egg—into the uterus of a woman. Our heart is like a uterus and we must allow the Lord to prepare it to receive His word. David said, *"Thy word have I hid in mine heart, that I might not sin against thee"* (Psalm 119:11). The word must be nurtured, protected and developed in us so that at the appointed time, it may burst forth in the birth of righteousness.

What I am saying is that sex and childbearing are symbols of God's love, desire for intimacy, and plan for our spiritual "childbearing" here on earth. God's command to Adam and Eve to *"be fruitful and multiply"* (Genesis 1:28), is echoed in Christ's admonition to his disciples that he has called them to *"bear much fruit"* (John 15:16). We also see God commanding the man to leave father and mother and cleave, or be joined to, his wife (Genesis 2:24) in the same way that Christ called his disciples out of the world to be one with him. But the parallel between marriage and Christ's relation to the church is unmistakable in the parable of the marriage supper. There is probably not one Bible scholar or theologian who doesn't see this parable in Matthew 22 and 25 as referring to Christ and the church. And just as Esther had to be prepared and adorned to enter into the king's bedchamber to be his wife, so too, the church is to be *"adorned as a bride for her husband"* (Revelation 21:2).

Those who are still having trouble with this concept of equating sexual union with the intimate union that God desires to have with His church, need only take a cursory read of *Song of Solomon*—a book long held by Biblical scholars to be an allegory of the love of Christ for his bride—to see that marriage, sex, conception and birth in the natural sphere were to be object lessons to teach about the spiritual realities of the relationship the believer has, or at least should have, with Christ. The Apostle Paul grasped this concept fully as he boldly told the Ephesians that marriage between a man and his bride is really only parable about the marriage between Christ and His church. After delineating how husbands and wives should live in harmonious relationship, he added: *"For this reason a man shall leave his father and mother and be joined to his wife, and the two shall become one flesh. This is a great mystery,* ***but I speak concerning Christ and the church****."* (Ephesians 5: 31, 32). He reminded the Romans that

"*...The righteousness of faith speaks in this way...The word is near you, even in your mouth and* ***in your heart****...* " (Romans 10:6, 8). Christ as our husband wants to plant his seed within us to be fertilized, nourished and birthed in good works. (Parables such as the sower and the seed (Matthew 13:4—8), the mustard seed (Matthew 13:31, 32), the leaven (Matthew 13:33), hint at this reality and are a prelude to the more direct teaching about this as revealed in passages such as John 15 where Jesus says that His followers are an extension and expression of Himself and where he warns that His word must abide ***in*** us if we are to bring forth and produce the works that would identify us as His.

Barrenness

Sometimes marriages are unfruitful. For some reason, the implantation of the seed into the woman does not bring about conception and birth. In spite of the promise of fruitfulness and the bearing of offspring, there are those marriages that remain childless, and this can be a source of great disappointment, frustration and alienation between the spouses. The Bible gives us glimpses of at least four marriages that suffered childlessness, and each is a portrait, of sorts, of what can happen in the marriage of the believer with Christ. These marriages were of devout, promise-keeping couples who were desirous of being fruitful but had their hopes and dreams frustrated. They were not persons who preferred childlessness to procreation. These were couples who felt a burden to bear children, precisely because they lived in the hope of birthing Messiah. So we must realize that barrenness can come to anyone, even the sincere and devoted child of God. But even to those who have every reason to expect fruitfulness because of the very special circumstances and promises surrounding their lives.

That is why *Don't Birth an Ishmael in the Waiting Room* examines the process by which a man or woman is separated from the world and his or her sin and brought into marital or intimate relationship with God and how the promise of fruitfulness may be tested through circumstances and delay before that word, conceived at conversion, fertilized by baptism and nurtured in the believer's heart, can be threatened by delay and aborted by unbelief and impatience. The promise is true. Its fertilization is guaranteed. But whether it bears fruit and is birthed in the life of the believer is very dependent on whether that believer is good soil. Just as the fertilized egg can be aborted in the mother's womb if conditions—her health, lifestyle, stress level and alimentation, to name a few—are not amenable to growth, so too the word conceived in the believer's heart can dry up and produce…nothing, if the believer's heart turns out to be poor soil for that word. In other words, as Bishop Joseph Northover has often said: "We place a great deal of emphasis on the seed, but the soil is of the utmost importance." That is why in Jesus' parable of the sower and the seed, He places the emphasis on the soil types and not on the seed as the determining factor whether or not there would be fruitfulness or barrenness in the life of the hearer or believer.

The first type of soil he refers to is the *wayside*. The seed that falls by the wayside is devoured by the fowls. Jesus described these believers as the ones that hear the word, but Satan comes immediately to snatch it away from them. The second is the *stony ground* where there isn't much earth. When the seed falls there, it springs up quickly. These people receive the word with gladness, but they have no root—no deep abiding faith—so they are offended, or turned off, when affliction and persecution arise on account of the word. In the realm of the spirit the enemy would love to keep us from conceiving by causing chaos and confusion. The third type of soil He calls *thorns and thistles,* which chokes the life out of the word. These people hear the word but the cares of the world, deceitfulness of riches and the lust of other things choke off the word and cause it to become unfruitful. The fourth place described by Jesus is *the good ground.* Not only does the good ground yield fruit, but there is also increase. It is fascinating to note that even the good ground yields different amounts of fruit, some thirty, some sixty, and some one hundred. Dr. Samuel N. Greene describes this as the thirty, sixty, and hundred fold Christians. This is symbolic of the different levels of faith and productiveness among the true believers, where maximum productivity is represented by the number one hundred. Whether a believer becomes fruitful or not is up to that believer's commitment to faith in Jesus Christ and His word.

As each believer peruses this book, it is necessary that he examines the lives of the Biblical characters presented to see whatever parallels exist between his and theirs, in order to learn from their mistakes and profit from their examples. Many of them birthed Ishmaels along the way, in different forms and under different circumstances. But whatever the differences, the underlying cause of the births of their Ishmaels was the same as Abraham and Sarah's: an impatience caused by God's delay, an encroaching despair and frustration that lead to a loss of faith in God's ability or willingness to bring forth the promise in their lives, and a taking into their own hands the birthing of that promise. The end result in each case was disastrous, for to birth an Ishmael is to actually hinder the purposes of God even while purporting to help in its furtherance. Whether the intent was a genuine attempt to speed up the birthing process, or whether it was selfishly and carnally motivated, but covered over with religious zeal, it really doesn't matter. The end result will always be the same: dishonor to God, obfuscation of His Divine purposes, and the birth of that which He cannot accept and the believer cannot use, to fulfill His Divine calling.

The first of these childless marriages we will look at is Hannah (I Samuel 1and 2). Hannah's barrenness burdened and frustrated her to the point of depression. It got to the point where she could not even worship. So intense was her depression that not even her husband's love could fill the void (I Samuel 1:8). She lost the joy of fellowship and praise, and worship became just one more occasion to face her childlessness. Finally, she cried out in her pain to the Lord for a child, promising to dedicate him as a Nazarite from birth. The purpose of her cry was to remove the reproach of her barrenness. And God came through for her, for the very next year she gave birth to Samuel who became one of the most influential prophets and judges of Israel. So if you are at a place of spiritual barrenness, know that prayer changes things. You don't pray to see if something happens, you pray so that something will happen. Pray and seek the Lord to determine if your conception is dependent on you dedicating your seed to the total honor and glory of God. God is able to open up a barren womb and cause it to be fruitful. You may be experiencing barrenness at the church you attend, the job where you work or the relationship you are in. The Lord may be trying to get your attention concerning the need for your unreserved dedication of your seed to His cause.

Rachel also experienced barrenness. In spite of Jacob's love for her and her desperate attempts to get pregnant, she remained fruitless. At one point she even entered into negotiation with her sister in her desperation, using superstitious means to accomplish that which only divine power can bring to pass. When Reuben found some mandrakes—believed to impart fertility to the womb—Rachel bargained with Leah for some. When even this did not work, she angrily blurted out to Jacob, "Give me children or I die!" (Genesis 30:1). Envy, desperation, anger, all proved useless in Rachel's bid to bear fruit from her womb. And again God comes through, for Genesis tells us that *"God remembered Rachel and listened to her and opened her womb."* (Genesis 30:22). Rachel needed to learn dependence and humility before she could birth the promise. She was impetuous, and idolatrous (See Genesis 31:34) but when she cried out in her need, God showed compassion. And He will do the same for all His children if they recognize their need and call to Him.

Another woman who found herself facing the spirit-crushing

stigma of barrenness was Rebekah. Married to Isaac the son of the promise, she found herself as dry as the hills of Gilboa. How ironic, to be the wife of the promised son whose very birth proclaimed the power of God to achieve the impossible, and whose very existence predicated the eventual birth of Messiah, and yet find yourself sterile and bare. No wonder Rebekah was filled with anguish and complained bitterly to the Lord about her faith-crushing situation. How is it possible that I am married to Isaac, the son of the promise and yet have no children? How can Messiah be born through Abraham's lineage through Isaac and I be unable to give birth? But while humanity could do nothing to bring forth seed, Divinity was waiting for the opportunity to turn barrenness into fruitfulness and give "beauty for ashes". The Scripture says that Isaac prayed for Rebekah's sterile womb and God heard and granted him his desire. Rebekah conceived and bore twins. Man's extremity is God's opportunity to show Himself gracious and kind to those in need, especially to His children whose faith is being stretched in the waiting room.

These three women suffered the anguish, embarrassment, promise-questioning and faith-destroying experience of childlessness. But each one learnt that her only help was in God and in due course received the hoped-for blessing by the providence of the Lord. Each one birthed a son who would go on to accomplish something great in the kingdom of God: Samuel became Israel's first prophet-priest, established the "schools of the prophet" and guided Israel's transition to a monarchy. Joseph went on to become Israel's preserver and an example to men everywhere of moral and spiritual integrity. Isaac would be used to give the world a glimpse of Messiah's submission to the Father's will and sacrificial death. But the next barren woman, Sarah, thought she had the solution to her barrenness and God's delay and in the process brought about one of the longest and strongest opposition to God's will in the world.

Sarah, like the other barren women in our study, felt the

anguish and experienced the doubt and embarrassment of her situation. As the years went by and the possibility of conception seemed ever more remote, she decided to take matters into her own hands and bring about that which God Himself had promised to do. She would add human works to God's promise in the hope of fulfilling God's promise. She would seek, through human means and reasoning to bring about the birth of an heir. She gave her Egyptian maid, Hagar, to Abraham. Now, from a mere human perspective, what she did was not wrong or unreasonable. After all, it was the custom and culture to do just what she did. As a matter of fact, it was considered the only right thing to do in cases like hers. But while she may have done what she did in order to provide an heir, her actions were prompted by doubt and disillusionment in God's plan. We know this by the fact that when the angel pronounced that she would bear a son the following year—this after Ishmael was already 12 years old— instead of praising God for the fulfillment of His promise, she laughed skeptically, muttering to herself, if she would have the pleasure of offspring being passed the time of productivity. (See Genesis 18: 10—15.) The angel had to reprimand her for her unbelief. And that is just the problem with the birth of Ishmael: it may have had the appearance of faith, but it was actually the result of doubt. It may have seemed to be the solution for the delay, but it was actually a cause for ***further*** delay. It may have stemmed from good intentions, but it brought only heartache, problems and a reproach of God's name. It may have seemed the most logical thing to do, but its lingering fallout—just witness the never-ending strife between Jews and Palestinians—defies all logic. Sarah thought the birth of Ishmael would have fulfilled God's promise and solved her problems. It only made them worse (See Genesis 16: 1—6; 21: 8—11). As a matter of fact, her experiment of mixing human works of doubt to the Divine word of faith and their disastrous results are the very basis for the title and thesis of this book. Just as Paul, years later, would refer to this "experiment" and use it as a lesson book of the futility of human efforts to fulfill Divine prerogatives, I, too, see it as a warning to today's Christians not to become impatient in the waiting room of God's supposed delay and try to hurry on the fulfillment of the promise and the word prophetically uttered over their lives.

Chapter 6
Lord, I'm Pregnant, Now What?

The parallel that exists between a pregnant woman and a believer who has been impregnated with purpose by God is amazing. Just as pregnancy develops through three trimesters, so too, one can envision a sort of tripartite development of this purpose and calling in the believer's experience. One of the greatest examples of His creative ability is the human body and its reproductive ability. Although the human body has millions of cells at birth, life begins when a single cell is created by the coming together of a sperm and an egg. Once the egg or the ovum is fertilized there is a pregnancy. As soon as the fertilization process took place which started your existence, a chemical change in the membrane surrounding the fertilized egg in your mother's womb stopped penetration by any other sperm. The Lord had you sealed from the time of your conception. Hallelujah!!

I can still recall the day my wife came home from the doctor's office and informed me that she was pregnant with our first child. O the joy, the excitement, the expectations, the dreams for this child to be born. I embraced her and we rejoiced in this happy event. But although I could rejoice with her, support her, give her encouragement and be by her side through the whole process, it was still hers, and hers alone to carry, nurture, protect and deliver the baby within her. Similarly, the believer must recognize that the seed [the calling, the promise] with which he or she has been impregnated is his or hers to bear, nurture and "bring to term". Others may be able to encourage and support, but the responsibility is the believer's to care for that word or promise, and in due time, bring it forth.

Pregnancy has its stages, which are divided into three trimesters. Each trimester has its characteristics and attendant challenges. For instance, in the first trimester, nausea is a problem. Fatigue can also be a factor, especially if the woman has small children or is working. Backaches occur due to the growth of the uterus, and as the spine adapts to the changing shape of the back. In the second trimester, her weight begins to increase as the fetus rises up into to the abdomen. She will also be able to hear the tiny heart beat of the fetus. She begins to feel more comfortable with her pregnancy as she fully embraces her role as expectant mother. Changes evident in the third trimester, such as continued weight gain, full breasts, and fetal movements and kicking, confirm to the woman that the fetus is thriving in her womb. These changes can bring great discomfort, not the least of which is her beginning to feel unattractive. Sexual relations are usually at a minimum at this stage for fear of hurting the fetus. Constipation, varicose veins, hemorrhoids, heartburn, and leg cramps are some of the other discomforts experienced at one stage or another during pregnancy.

In like manner, the gestation of the word, the promise, the calling in the believer's "pregnancy" has its stages with their attendant problems and characteristics. For just as the physiological, physical and emotional changes in a pregnant woman are readily discernible and become more and more evident as the pregnancy progresses, there should be tangible evidence of spiritual changes in the life of the "pregnant" believer. Take Joseph, for example. He was impregnated with the promise of headship. As the implanted seed was fertilized by his two dreams, little did he expect to go through the three stages of its gestation. And each stage had its own challenges, just like the pregnant woman. First, like those barren women who feel strong jealousy and anger towards other women who get pregnant, the believer has to beware of those who would seek to abort his pregnancy by their cynicism, gossip, slander and sabotaging efforts. Often these "abortionists" are other Christians who are still in the waiting room of barrenness, who can't understand why they remain fruitless while the believer has conceived. Do you remember Sarai's attitude towards Hagar when she became pregnant for Abraham? Or Hannah's towards Penninah? It was jealousy about Joseph's impregnation that lead his brothers to try to kill the dream by first deciding to kill him, but afterwards, deciding to sell Joseph as a slave. Thus he went from a pit—first trimester, to a prison—second trimester, to a palace—third trimester. I can just imagine the literal nausea he must have felt when he was thrown into that pit and then as he rode off, a slave, into the unknown. The fatigue he must have felt as he began to take in this new situation in his life and tried to cope must have been difficult, indeed. He must have experienced mood swings as the realization that he might never see his father again began to dawn on him. Joseph experienced in his spiritual pregnancy the aches, pains, fatigue, doubt, sensitivity and occasional frustration experienced by most pregnant women as he progressed through each stage of the gestation of his dream. But one thing was sure: the dream was being fulfilled as each new difficulty and challenge came up. It was developing, taking form, having its components put in place so that when the moment arrived for its birthing, it would be a live, healthy, well-formed and thriving "baby". And God is perfecting something great in the life of every dedicated believer that will make all the difficulties and challenges of "pregnancy" worthwhile. Not only will you birth the vision God has in you; you will see its completion and perfection because it is a holy thing. Paul told the Philippians that a good work was begun in them and it would be performed until the day of the Lord Jesus (See Philippians 1:6). Through continual fasting, prayer, worship, and studying of the word—the alimentation of the soul—remember, pregnant women need to eat well so they will be adequately nourished to sustain the life growing within them—your promise, your word will develop into what God has envisioned for you, into perfection and completion.

The last trimester is often the most difficult. There is great discomfort, the fatigue of the first trimester returns, indigestion, heartburn and difficulty sleeping. Greatest of all is the feeling of wanting it all to be done with, or being impatient to deliver the baby. The pain is usually greatest right before the birthing as contractions increase and the uterus moves toward full dilation. The baby kicks more now and harder. He, too, it seems, can hardly wait to get out. Again looking at the lives of those who were about to birth their purpose, we see this parallel trend: Joseph was forgotten by the butler who had promised to intercede with Pharaoh on his behalf; David was so worn out by the repeated attacks from Saul that he despaired of life and decided to go into the land of the Philistines; Jesus sweated drops of blood in the Garden of Gethsemane as He prepared to drink from the bitter cup that opened the door for our salvation. All of this happened at the point of breakthrough. It was as the old adage goes: it is always darkest just before dawn. So don't be surprised or discouraged if, after all your waiting and nurturing of your dream and vision, just as you are about to bring it to fruition, you see opposition and experience setbacks. That might be the very indication that you are about to give birth. What are you experiencing now that you're in the latter stage of your pregnancy? Do you feel forgotten like Joseph, abandoned at the very point where it looked like everything was finally falling in place? Are you, like David, suffering repeated attacks, wondering what you are doing in a cave with bats over your head and death chasing you, when all you have done is faithfully serve your King? And are you "sweating drops of blood" like Jesus as you seem to have to carry on all alone in the "Garden", trying to reconcile your will to God's at this place where there should be roses but all you can see are thorns and thistles? Be encouraged, all these are just birth pangs. Do not become weary. The time of your delivery is near. Remember, Jesus said you will reap in due season if you faint not. This is your season. This is your hour. Allow the Holy Spirit to strengthen you. Brace yourself. You are about to give birth to that which God has placed in you. The time has come for that which is in you to come out of you. It is time for the vision to be fulfilled; the plan to become an accomplishment; the dream to become a reality. For unto you, yes you, a child is about to be born!

CHAPTER 7
HELP MY WATER BROKE! GET THIS BABY OUT!

"For the children are come to the birth, and there is not strength to bring forth" (2 Kings 19:3b).

I have often spoken to women in the last trimester, especially those in the 8th or 9th month. They are engorged, uncomfortable and desperate to deliver. They speak about just wanting to push the child out, to be over and done with the pregnancy. After all, they have carried this child for the past nine months. They have nurtured him from the very stores of their own body. They have suffered all the health challenges of being pregnant and endured the discomfiture. They have even abstained from sexual pleasure just to ensure the wellbeing of the unborn child. But now they want to see, hold, love and care for this developing child in the real world. They want to get on with the new phase of their lives. Well, "pregnant" believer, you will also get to the point where you havc to break forth with your promise, when you must bring to birth. You persevered in the waiting room and finally became pregnant by your word from the Lord which has fully developed in your uterus [heart]. This is no Ishmael that is about to be born. No, this is the "child of promise". This is your Divine purpose that you have carried to term and are now waiting to deliver. Just as every woman will experience the breaking of her water bag, you, too will see your water break. The hour of delivery has come and it is time to strengthen yourself and bring forth the vision the Lord impregnated you with in the secret place of worship.

But the olive has to be crushed in order to expel the oil. The coal has to go through pressure to become a diamond, Gold has to be placed in the fire to remove the dross, and you have to be afflicted to walk in your anointing. God brought you into this year, the year of birthing and finality, and you must not allow the spirit of procrastination to keep you from birthing your purpose. Sarai received strength from God to conceive and you will need His strength to deliver or you run the risk of becoming like the children in Hezekiah's day that "*came to the birth but had no strength to deliver*" (I Kings 19: 3). Delivery has its own problems and difficulties, and until that baby is out and the umbilical cord cut, the birthing process isn't over. Even at the point of delivery, a baby can be aborted, hurt in the delivery process, or even arrive still born. Besides that, the mother herself can die in the delivery of her child, like Rachel and Phinehas' wife did (Genesis35: 16—18; I Samuel 4: 19, 20). Ironically, these children who should have been children of promise, whose births should have heralded great joy and expectation, became symbols of God's aborted plan for Israel, symbols of how things can go wrong and blessings can be lost. Their very names cry out to the disenchantment of their mothers. Rachel called her son Benoni, *son or my mourning,* while Phinehas' wife named hers Ichabod, *the glory has departed.* So you, dear believer cannot take for granted that the word implanted, gestated will automatically, easily, and without pain be brought forth to life. You cannot afford, even at this late stage, to become careless or complacent with the purpose and vision that has been nurtured and cherished and brought to the point of delivery. There must be strength to deliver, a strength that will only come from continued vigilance, prayer and diligence, for even at this stage, there are still trials and hardships to endure. And as the woman in travail must push to deliver, so too, you must push to deliver your purpose, dream, vision, calling. In this, your year of fruitfulness, you must push beyond adversity and disappointment; push beyond mediocrity and complacency; push beyond back-biters and criticizers; push beyond jealous haters and saboteurs trying to still-born your vision; push beyond enmities and envy of those who see the hand of God's favor on your life. Push. Push. Push.

You resisted the devil's attempt to cause spontaneous and induced "abortion" while you were in the waiting room because you knew God had impregnated you with purpose. You endured the "nausea and the morning sickness", and you refused to abort when the enemy tried to tell you that there might be "birth defects" or other complications if you decided to carry the "pregnancy" to term. You didn't birth a preemie in the waiting room by stepping out before your time. You patiently endured the hardship of your pregnancy and allowed God to develop the "fetus" He planted in you. It would be very devastating to come this far and not deliver the baby, or deliver one that is stillborn.

Now, returning to the birthing of your vision. There are many believers sitting in churches at the latter part of the "third trimester". The "baby" is fully developed but instead of preparing to step out they just sit because they don't want to leave their covering without the right hand of blessing. They are waiting for their divinely appointed mentor to recognize that they are ready to birth their own ministry, and as a skilled midwife, help them "deliver" it. But this does not happen, so they go through the motions of ministry, unhappy, unfulfilled, and anxious for release, like the mother who feels like her pregnancy will never end and becomes "antsy" and miserable. They want to birth their ministry, sensing that their *kairos*—appointed— moment has arrived, but their "midwife" is missing in action. They feel they can't go it alone and are afraid that, without the approval, blessing and unstinting support of their "covering' they will fail because they ran ahead. To those in such a situation, I say, "Just as the pregnant woman's body gives indications that delivery is imminent, and she begins to bear down in labor—sometimes in the back seat of a car, or in an elevator, at a family function, usually with no medical personnel around, but still manages to bring forth a healthy baby; As a matter of fact, no matter how inconvenient the time or place, once those contractions begin, no one can stop her from having her baby. You will know if your time has come by the moving of your spirit and the alignment of providence.

If the 'baby' God has placed in you has matured under the leadership of your covering, and you sense that now is delivery time, push it out, step out to your calling and purpose, with or without a "midwife". If you've been faithful to the local house, spending the necessary time in the waiting room patiently allowing the baby to develop, don't fear birthing an Ishmael. Fear not moving at your *kairos* moment. Fear stagnation and death of your vision and ministry. Fear not trusting the anointing that breaks the yoke. Fear not stepping out in faith and with God. You don't have to cause a scene nor separate with acrimony. You don't have to burn the bridge you once crossed on. But you do have to move on. Like Rebekah who respectfully refused to linger on in her father's home once she recognize divine providence had marked her for a different life as Isaac's wife, in spite of her mother's and brother's request for her to "*remain with us ten days or so"* (Genesis 24:55), say your loving goodbyes, get on your "camel" and head out for the new life God has designated for you.

Travail To Prevail

"A woman when she is in travail hath sorrow, because her hour is come: but as soon as she is delivered of the child, she remembereth no more the anguish, for joy that a man is born into the world. And ye now therefore have sorrow: but I will see you again, and your heart shall rejoice, and your joy no man taketh from you." (John 16:21-22). Labor is not for the faint of heart and

that is the reason most believers stay on the periphery of the faith. But to know the mysteries of the Kingdom and dwell in the secret place, the believer must be willing to travail. Paul continually "*travailed in childbirth*" (Galatians 4:19) until Christ was formed in the Galatians. Christ travailed in the Garden of Gethsemane until He prevailed against the enemy who wanted Him to pass the cup of bitterness He drank for our sweet salvation. John travailed on the island of Patmos and there gave us God's glorious revelation of Christ's return. Jacob travailed at the brook Peniel and there saw the face of God and had his name changed. But travailing isn't easy, neither there be birth without the labor pains associated with it. If travailing was easy then every believer would birth a vision, or bring forth fruit for the Kingdom. However, only those willing and prepared to endure the suffering of the labor room will experience the joys associated with bringing forth a child.

Many believers have no concept of what it means to travail: in early morning prayer, in fasting—to turn down their plates and afflict their flesh through self denial, in radical worship that takes the believer into the secret place to be overshadowed by His Glorious Presence, in denying earthly lusts and seeking divine purity. Instead they seek to enter the Kingdom on a bed of ease, ignoring that the very word says that it is through much hardships that we enter into life. These stony ground Christians look at the chaste lifestyle of the steadfast believer and respond to their self denial by saying, "it don't take all that." What a pity they don't know that it takes all that and then some to walk in the supernatural realm. Christ is our example and He paid the ultimate price to birth our salvation. We, too, have to pay the price to birth out an anointing. We must endure the birth pangs for that which God has formed in us to manifest itself through us.

You may be experiencing hard labor and sorrow now but Jesus said the woman forgets her sorrow once she is delivered; she forgets her anguish and feels joy because a man is born into the world. Jesus used the analogy of a woman in travail to explain to the disciples that they would suffer like a woman in travail once He was taken away, but their suffering would lead to joy because they would see Him again. In the same way, the joy of having birthed your purpose will obscure the memory of any suffering or hardship borne in bringing it to be.

But what is this travailing of which we speak? Well, Jesus said it to His disciples when He was on earth and its sentiments reverberate down through the ages to us today. He said, *"If any man would come after me, let him deny himself, take up his cross and follow me."* (Luke 9: 23). The first aspect of our travailing is self-denial. If we are to follow on to know the Lord then we have to be willing to deny our flesh the ungodly things it craves. The second is the willingness to take up our cross. There is no work we can do to earn our salvation since Jesus already paid the price for our salvation once and for all on Calvary. However, we must endure trials and tribulations as we stand for Him in a dark world. The third thing we must do is follow Him: on the path of service and humility. Follow Him in strict obedience to the Father's will. Follow Him even if it means giving our lives to advance the Kingdom agenda in this world.

Whatever the travail you are experiencing now, it is perfecting you and taking you to a place of fruitfulness. Is it persecution? Then it is part of the process for Christ to be formed in us. Have you suffered abandonment by a husband or a wife? Have you lost a loved one? Or perhaps you are suffering from a debilitating disease, or are in a deep economic crisis. Whatever the travail, find a way to know the Christ who is a very present help in the crisis, and receive an anointing in your affliction. Your Father in heaven is your "obstetrician", and while He will not exempt you from the birth pangs, be confident that He will see and guide you through the delivery. The Father asks, *"Shall I bring to the birth and not cause to bring forth? saith the LORD: shall I cause to bring forth, and shut the womb? saith thy God"* (Isaiah 66:9). God has caused your "cervix" to be fully dilated because He expects you to bring forth. God will not waste His seed. He does not impregnate with purpose to shut the womb. He has brought you to the birth and will not allow anything to interfere with your delivery. Jesus will not allow the thief to kill, steal or destroy the seed planted and nurtured in you, so stop worrying. What is yours is yours. The door of opportunity that God has opened cannot be closed by anyone. (See Revelation 3: 7, 8.)

You've been in the waiting room a long time but your travail won't be long because, *"For as soon as Zion travailed, she brought forth her children."* (Isaiah 66:8). Zion is not bringing a child, she is bringing forth children. The birthing of God's vision for your life is laborious because it is multifaceted and not one dimensional. This is why your labor pains have you feeling like you are pregnant with triplets. There can be no bringing forth without a travailing. The irony is, while the waiting might have been long, as soon as it is over, things move pretty quickly.

Purpose In Your Pain: Your Labor Is Not In Vain

In the natural, a woman's mental state can influence the course of her labor, and the same is true for every believer that is ready to give birth. In natural childbirth the woman who is relaxed and enthusiastic during labor is better able to tolerate discomfort and work with the process. On the contrary, anxiety can increase her perception of pain and reduce her tolerance of it. Anxiety and fear can cause the secretion of stress compounds from the adrenal glands. These compounds inhibit uterine contractions and divert blood flow from the placenta. Keep in mind it is the uterine contractions and the woman's timely pushing that facilitates the birth. Therefore, anything that causes anxiety or stress, any fear or foreboding harbored in your spirit will inhibit your ability to "contract your uterine muscles" and push in a timely manner. As you are about to deliver remember, *"God hath not given us the spirit of fear; but of power, and of love, and of a sound mind" (2 Timothy 1:7).* At this stage of your experience, you should be past the "what if" syndrome of second guessing yourself and God's leading in your endeavors. At this late stage of your "pregnancy" your water had already broke so you must prepare yourself to push the baby out now. After the water breaks, any delay in getting the baby out leads to a "dry birth" and dry births are always more difficult and painful. Perhaps you may need to borrow some money to purchase equipment, or move to another state to begin your ministry, or accept that invitation to work in the mission field, or finally say yes to that marriage proposal. Now is not the time to be "wondering or vacillating". If you miss your *kairos* moment, your golden opportunity, you may have to work even harder and suffer even more setbacks, when you do decide to move forward. No matter what you do, there will be travailing to bring to birth, so just prepare yourself for the labor pains associated with your childbirth and, as I said before…Push. And just in case you feel you can't make it, look around you at the great cloud of witnesses in the birthing room with you, encouraging you to bring the baby forth. These witnesses are the faithful men and women who have gone through the conception, carrying and delivering of their "babies" before you, whose testimonies validate God's promise to see you through. Just look around you to the ministries of men like T.D. Jakes, who left Virginia and moved to Texas to begin the Potter's House Ministry. Or women like Juanita Bynum who left her job as a flight attendant to embark on her prophetic ministry. And what can we say of people like Eddie Long of Atlanta, or Joel Osteen of Texas, Dr. Samuel N. Greene of Narrow Way Ministries or any of the countless men and women who felt the call, were impregnated with a vision of their mission and purpose, nurtured that vision, served with and under others of greater experience, saw that vision grow and take form in their spirits, and then, when the *kairos* moment arrived, they stepped out and stepped forward to birth their ministries. It wasn't easy for them, but they didn't abort and they didn't quit because they knew the pain would give way to joy. And just look at them today. Let their testimony be your motivation not to give up or give in.

CHAPTER 8
THE BABY IS HERE! NOW WHAT?

We pray for promotion and increase; we pray for the ability to birth a vision but do we realize that inherent in promotion and increase, and the birthing of a vision are many challenges? Does the excitement of birthing blind us to the need for proper preparation once the baby arrives, and of the ebbs and flows, the highs and lows that are attendant to its arrival and care?

There are countless women who desire to give birth but who are not ready to deal with the emotional roller coaster of dealing with a new born. As a matter of fact, this roller coaster of emotion can be as grave as post-partum blues, where the mother will go through periods when she feels let down, disappointed and even acrimonious toward her newborn child who has brought so many changes to her life. My wife once told me about a mother who left her baby on the couch and locked herself in the bedroom because the baby would not stop crying. Khadija Johnson, my dear sister in the Lord, also shared with me her personal experience of post partum blues: *"After giving birth to my daughter, as I was sitting on the hospital bed calling everyone I could think of to celebrate my joyous experience of giving birth, I started feeling alone and abandoned. I felt no one cared because I could not reach anyone. Because I was feeling rejected I then started to reject the very thing I had given birth to. Because I felt that no one wanted me, or cared for me, I carried that feeling over to my daughter and it took me a long time to love her."* But post partum depression and post partum psychosis are even more dangerous than post partum blues because they impair the mother's perception of reality. As hard as this might be to believe, my wife also told me of the case of a woman who thought her baby looked like a snake and was ready to throw it out the window.

The minister who has birthed a new ministry is also not exempt from his or her own bout with post partum blues. He or she will go through periods of feeling let down and abandoned as they try to adapt to the changes that the ministry has brought to their life, especially if it seems as though they are dealing with everything by themselves. It horrifies us when we hear that a mother has done something terrible to her baby because we assume that all women are equipped to nurture the baby and handle the stress associated with the constant attention a baby requires. But the stress that child bearing can place on a mother's emotional and psychological reserves are so tremendous, sometimes it short-circuits that very natural nurturing instinct. So it should not surprise us when individuals who have given birth to ministries find themselves in a similar situation. A young ministry can tax a minister's spiritual, emotional and even physical reserves almost to the breaking point. Often that minister has to do almost everything as many of the members are new to Christianity themselves and are unable to contribute much to the ministry's survival and success. Many times these ministries are in rental spaces and the equipment must be moved and transported before and after every meeting. Financial means are often low and the minister must not only work a "9 to 5", but also deal with all the problems and issues of this nascent ministry. Then one day we see a successful ministry with all its auxiliaries but have no clue about the tears cried, the last dollar spent, or the feelings of abandonment felt by the person the Lord used to birth it.

And yet there are some of us who have the audacity to criticize a pastor when his or her ministry flourishes. We make comments like "Look at that car. Look at those suits. Did you see those expensive shoes?" But where were we when the "baby" needed feeding, and cleaning? When tiredness gnawed at the very soul of the pastor and his resources were exhausted providing for the nurture and upkeep of this now flourishing ministry? Yes, we see the baby when it is dressed in pink or blue, when it smells sweet from the baby oil and the powder, and sits quietly and charmingly in its crib because it is well fed, but do we empathize with the mom, especially that single mom that is at the breaking point trying to do her best? We see the glory, but do we know the story? Do we even care to know?

I cannot emphasize enough the importance of preparation for the birthing of one's purpose and vision. That is why the stay in the waiting room of preparation is so critical. If the people who do their full term in the waiting room for every level of promotion still struggle as they nurture their baby, how much more the individual who gives birth without proper preparation? People doted on you when you were pregnant but now that you have delivered you better expect and be ready for the changes and the challenges of raising the child.

Once the baby arrives you must be ready for the lack of sleep because you have to wake up at weird hours to feed the baby. People will want to hold and cuddle the baby when it is young, but who will change the diapers, clean the vomit and be willing to baby-sit once the infant begins to reach "the terrible two's" or the "treacherous three's"? Your life is not the same now that you have birthed and your time in the waiting room was to prepare you for that reality. When you give birth before you are able to care for a baby, the responsibility for its care falls on others. The baby of one becomes the burden of another and its beauty is lost because of the lack of preparedness of the one who birthed it. So while you must step out without delay when the time is ripe, don't be cajoled or coerced into stepping out before you are ready.

Don't be like the many people who are convinced by others

that stepping out in ministry is simply a matter of renting a building and starting a church. Then those same people who inveigled and persuaded them to do so and were oh so happy at the outset—just like those who share the joys of child birth with the new mom and dad—soon disappear leaving the man or woman of God to handle the responsibility of paying the rent and all the other bills and responsibilities associated with the building. They don't show up for services, or if they do they are late and nonchalant. But the leader has to show up whether or not the people do. The message has to be preached whether to one or one thousand. The leader has to handle all the challenges that accompany the birthing of the ministry. The situation is especially egregious in this era of church hopping. People like the euphoria of going to a ministry they've never gone to before and enjoying the "newness", but the test is how long will they stay. Some of them tell the leader that the Lord sent them to assist and that they are there for the long haul, but as soon as their flesh gets chastened, they jump ship and head to another church. These people come with an agenda. They come seeking a position, a pulpit and a public. Thus the pastor is now on a timetable. He or she has a time limit. "Look at me. Use me or lose me." A man of God once told me that "some people that show up at a church are other churches' rejects." They tore up the last church they were at. They caused a split and then split. Maybe résumés and references should be requested when an individual shows up at a church claiming to be a minister. How many of them would like to have their former leader called for a reference? It is worth repeating that nurturing a newborn is very challenging and requires great sacrifice. It is not enough to not birth an Ishmael, it is also necessary to care for the Isaac that has been given.

Life will never be the same after the birth of a child. The carefree attitude and flexibility one had before are now things of the past. Now everything has to be channeled through the needs of the baby. Schedules have to be rearranged. Financial priorities have to be adjusted. Relaxation and recreation have to be made subservient to the nurturing of the baby and the younger the baby, the more constant the care that has to be given. When necessity demands that the parent must leave the child, the great concern must be to ensure that the babysitter is someone of integrity who will take care of that child with the same watchfulness and attention that the parent would. Similarly, the leader of the new vision birthed by the Lord must exercise discernment when it comes to leaving their baby in the care of someone else. Babysitters have been caught on camera doing cruel things to the baby in their charge. What is your babysitter doing to your baby when you are not around? There are a lot of people that would love to kidnap your baby and claim it as their own. Those who would seek to exploit your absence to their own benefit by seeking to turn your flock against you and to themselves, as when Absalom stole the hearts of the men of Israel from his father David. And there are others who don't want your ministry; they just want to hurt it when you're not around because of the envy that has risen up in their hearts because of your fruitfulness. Then there are those who are like the woman in the story of Solomon and the two women who claimed that a particular baby belonged to each of them. (I Kings 3: 16—26). The baby of one of the mothers had died and she snatched the other mother's baby while she was sleeping and replaced it with her dead baby. The mother of the live baby said to King Solomon, *"and we were together; there was no stranger with us in the house, save we two in the house."* (1 Kings 3:18). Rise from the spirit of sleep and slumber and discern who is in the house with you. We get so concerned about a stranger kidnapping the baby that we sometimes forget that the danger is in the house. Molestation is often committed by a member of the family; someone of the very household the child belongs to. The woman who stole the baby was willing to see the baby cut in half in order to settle the matter. She didn't go through the morning sickness, the kicks at night, no backaches, no dreaming and talking to the belly. Thus she didn't care whether it lived or not. There are people whose vision is dead and because they didn't go through what you went through to birth that "baby", they want yours to die as well. You carried the baby to term and endured the labor pains to bring it into the world, so don't be surprised when others aren't as enthusiastic as you are about its growth and development. Sometimes the people that treat your "baby", your vision, the worst are family members. Some men and women of God will tell you that the greatest opposition they received in the birthing of the church came from family members. Every conscientious servant of God will be watchful and discerning concerning who they let stand by their side in ministry, or who they cede leadership to in their times of absence.

David was driven to the brink of despair because of Saul's jealousy. *"And David said in his heart, I shall now perish one day by the hand of Saul: there is nothing better for me than that I should speedily escape into the land of the Philistines; and Saul shall despair of me, to seek me any more in any coast of Israel: so shall I escape out of his hand"* (1 Samuel 27:1). And you will have to deal with the same spirit of jealousy that will take hold of people when your baby or your vision is birthed. Many of them would have abandoned the waiting room of preparation, acted in the flesh and birthed an Ishmael that was rejected by God. Now they are hoping that you will fail too because misery loves company. Don't allow their jealous attacks to depress you and cause you to despise or abandon the "baby". And there will be times when like David you will have to encourage yourself in the Lord because some of the very people who celebrated you when you got "pregnant" and gave birth to your ministry will be the same ones saying, "Why did you get "pregnant" if you knew you couldn't afford it? Why did you get the building if you knew you could not afford it? You should have thought of that before." You and they have to understand that there are unforeseen situations and circumstances with every child that will challenge and confound you as a parent.

Chapter 9
Who Dropped You?

> *"And Jonathan, Saul's son, had a son that was lame of his feet. He was five years old when the tidings came of Saul and Jonathan out of Jezreel, and his nurse took him up, and fled: and it came to pass, as she made haste to flee, that he fell, and became lame. And his name was Mephibosheth"* (2 Samuel 4:4).

The incident of Mephibosheth and his nurse is a warning to everyone who has given birth of how, in a moment of crisis, that child can be dropped and injured for life. With the great upheaval that the death of Saul and Jonathan brought, the young nurse in charge of Mephibosheth took him up to flee with him to safety, but in her haste and anxiety, she dropped him and he became a lifelong cripple after that. The irony of it is that she had taken him up to protect and save him. Her intentions were noble. Her actions were laudable, but yet she dropped him causing him lifelong damage. In circumstances like these, it is easy to throw blame and criticize and "Monday-morning-quarterback" the situation. Yes, she was responsible for his becoming a cripple but she is not to blame because she was doing the best she could under the circumstances. Everybody thinks that the other person should have done more to avoid a bad situation or to encourage a good one until faced with similar challenges and ending up with similar results. So, Pastor, if you think your ministry is still at its delicate and vulnerable stage and can ill-afford to be dropped, it may be best not to absent yourself, or give control to someone else, just in case. After all, you don't want to find yourself in a situation where, should things go bad, you must live with the nagging feeling that if you were present or at the helm, things would have turned out better, that your ministry would not have been "dropped".

There are many adults, lame and emotionally crippled, who were dropped as children and never recovered. They are still dazed and confused from that one incident that turned their life upside down. And whether it was intentionally done or not, the result is still the same: lame in the feet, crippled for effective service. Perhaps you, dear reader, are one of the dropped ones. You are still limping about emotionally, still bearing in your soul the devastation of that "fall". So, like my friend Eileen is wont to ask, "Who dropped you?" Who was that trusted person that let you fall? Who was that person responsible for your wellbeing and safety who ended up crippling you? Who is to blame for your sorry condition? Or are they? Have you given thought to the fact that perhaps they did the best that they could under the circumstances? Have you considered that they might have been actually seeking your best good when they "dropped" you? Perhaps it was a single, unwed mom who gave you up for adoption or left you at Aunt Sue's for the holidays and never came back. Have you considered that she might have done so because she knew she couldn't take care of you and felt that you stood a better chance at Aunt Sue? Or maybe it was a pastor who gave some advice that didn't turn out the way it was supposed to. Have you given thought to the many hours he spent with you, comforting and encouraging you when you were down? And what about the fact that he is only human and had no way of anticipating the unforeseen forces that invalidated his, at the time, wise counsel? Or perhaps it was a brother or sister in the church who didn't come through for you as you expected. Have you taken into account that they might have run into insurmountable obstacles that prevented them from doing for you what they had planned? Yes, they are responsible for "dropping" you and causing you some serious, and in some cases, irreparable hurt, but are they really to blame? Think about it. Would you have done better given the same circumstances and mitigating factors?

But let us say you were "dropped" maliciously and willfully by someone who gained your trust and then betrayed it: like the friend of mine who, after having cultivated a deep friendship with his pastor, and having given much time, effort and money to build the ministry was shunted aside and publicly humiliated when the pastor listened to unsubstantiated rumors about him and never once asked him if they were true; or the many youth who have been physically molested by their clergy, who decided to *prey* but not to *pray*; or the children sexually molested by their parents, some of them leaders in their churches. As hard as it is to be "dropped", especially when it has been so devastating, it is still time to stop doling out blame and start sharing forgiveness. No amount of recrimination will change the facts of the situation nor make your life better again. So you might as well deal with it and move on. Do you want to remain a Mephibosheth, an emotional and spiritual quadriplegic, unable to navigate the obstacle courses of life, or "*run the race that is set before [you]*?" (Hebrews 12:1).

In some cases you may need to seek professional help and find a spiritual partner to help you through the dark days and frightful nights. If you find yourself reliving again and again the incidents of the past that scarred your soul, finding it difficult, if not impossible to commit to any ministry or anyone, then you definitely need to find a Godly counselor and release those toxic memories. If you find yourself living the very accursed life that you despise—like being a closet homosexual or lesbian or drug addict—it is time to come out of the closet by seeking a trusted soul who can become your accountability partner and help you through the maze of sin. Or maybe you were "dropped" by an ex-husband or wife who took your best years and walked out on you after years of marriage. You bent over backwards to please your spouse and make the marriage work and now you are left an emotional train wreck, battling low self-esteem and a spirit of suicide because after suffering so many years of emotional abuse you have nothing left. And now you find yourself unable to function normally in another relationship because your ex is "still with you", preventing you from giving yourself in true love to your new spouse. You need to come clean and be transparent with your new spouse if healing is to be complete. I am not saying that it will be easy to recover from having been dropped. But what I am saying is that it is necessary, for your own peace and prosperity, and for the purpose that God has birthed within you.

The most effective way to combat your having been "dropped" is to be vigilant with the "Isaac" that you have birthed. Remember it was the person responsible for your wellbeing who, maliciously or not, dropped you and caused you to walk through life crippled and ineffective. Now that God has redeemed your life and given you a place of honor—like David did for Mephibosheth (See II Samuel 9:9—12)—do not make the same mistake that was made with you. Care well for your ministry and the lambs that have been placed in your charge. Watch out for the Ishmaels who will try to molest and tease and mock the Isaacs under your care. (See Genesis 21: 7—9). Like Sarah, you will have to stand firm in banishing the Ishmaels from the camp. After all, Isaac is your baby, your son of the promise. You waited a long time to receive him from the Lord. At times you almost lost faith in the promise; you were even tempted to birth your own Ishmael because of the frustration. But now, here he is, beautiful and full of life, weaned but not yet able to fend for himself. He still needs your vigilant watch care and nurturing. He is depending on you for healthy growth and development. You cannot afford to "drop" this child of promise, so do your duty and care for this "child". Sarah was adamant, *"Get rid of that slave woman and her son."* (Genesis 21:10). The Ishmaels of the world can never and should never be made to share in the inheritance of the Isaacs of the world. It just can't happen, so watch out and take care and don't "drop" your Isaac. Now your Isaac might be a special sense of calling and vision for a work that the Lord wants to do through you, or it might be a fledgling ministry, or a young convert God has placed under your mentorship, or your own biological seed. It really doesn't matter. The principle remains the same: Take care of that which the Lord has birthed in and through you, for its prosperity and effectiveness are dependent on your diligence.

APPENDIX

Personal Testimonies From Individuals Who Were Dropped.

Tasha's Testimony

Being dropped whether you drop yourself or if someone has dropped you can be a devastating or crippling experience, if it is not dealt with, it can stay with you as you live your life.

I've been dropped many times in many different ways at different stages of my life. I want to share some of these times with you to let you know that no matter what anyone or "anything" tells you, you are not the only one that has ever been dropped. What really makes the difference between some people and others is your reaction and how you deal with it when you are in the "dropped" stage.

To begin with I was adopted at the age of 8 months. I have always known that I was adopted. I was told by my adopted parents that my biological mother was very young when she had me and that she herself went through a stage of giving me up and then taking me back, finally giving me up for adoption at 8 months old. I am the oldest of now 6 children and 3 are from different countries of the world. The next to be adopted was my brother from Vietnam, and then my sister from Cambodia, then my parents had my two sisters who weren't adopted, (two more brothers were adopted from India but after I had left home). We were known as the "unusual international family" especially in the fact that we all grew up in a town where this is not the "normal family". Everyone had been amazed by our family. We were interviewed and had an article with pictures displayed in Massachusetts's Boston's Children's Museum for years.

We did not struggle financially growing up. We traveled every summer for vacation to many different places. My parents believed in educating us about different cultures to show us there were people that were not as privileged as we were. We went to every museum in the surrounding states. My parents believed in reading books instead of watching TV and if we were to watch TV it would be documentaries. National Geographic became my best friend! While other kids my age were watching Saturday morning cartoons we were outside mowing the lawn or cutting down trees as we lived on quite a bit of land. My parents encouraged us to take up instruments and learn new things (I think I took lessons for just about every instrument there is to take). I took horse back riding lessons, then took English dressage lessons. I did horse shows and entered jumping competitions. I remember asking for a horse and 3 months later my dad and I built a two story barn for 2 horses. Two months after there were two horses in the barn. One of the horses was a Morgan show horse and the other we actually traveled to the island of wild horses called Chincoteague, in Virginia. In Chincoteague they drove wild ponies across once a year for an auction. My parents actually took all of us there to buy a pony that I picked out. I trained the pony that summer so that my sister could ride it.

My parents didn't believe in having all the electronics that everyone else that I knew had. We only had one TV, one radio and one record player. They encouraged us to do things that we showed interest in. Inside of me I always had a hard time feeling like I fit in, like I belonged. I didn't feel loved. I had a difficult time expressing what I was feeling on the inside to anyone. My mother told me that when I was a baby I would have screaming fits if they tried to place me on the floor; I always wanted to be held. I had a very difficult time with rejection (I didn't want to be rejected at any level) I didn't like myself and I felt like I had no self-worth. I felt like I didn't deserve anything. I grew up with the thoughts of why my biological mother would want to give me up? What was wrong with me that caused her to give me up for adoption? I couldn't understand this; it didn't make any sense to me. I was DROPPED! It didn't matter that some one had gone through all the problems of actually adopting me.

Adoption is a very long process and can take years if you do so internationally. Though I was born outside of Boston, Massachusetts it was still a long process. What I kept thinking in the back of my mind was she didn't want to keep me, and there must be something wrong with me. I wanted so much to be accepted by anyone because that to me at the time would give me that couple of minutes of being accepted (what a dangerous place to be!). In Elementary school I tried my best to be liked by everyone. When someone got mad with me it was absolutely devastating to me and I would close myself in my room for days. In high school this happened as well. In 9th grade I closed myself off from the whole family for a month barely talking to anyone except for the necessary communications with the family, all because a girl at school told me she didn't like me. My parents didn't know what to do so they sent me to boarding school. They thought this would help the situation and enable me to be able to meet new people as I was starting to hang around the wrong crowd. Well, it did not help the situation it made it worse, only because I felt on the inside that my parents were trying to get rid of me. It felt like I was being punished and yet again being given away and I resented them for it. This didn't help the relationship that I had with my parents at all. I felt like no one understood me. It was the root of being in abusive relationships, as well as it opened the door for many other issues that followed me through the years!

Another major drop came when I left my parents house. At that time I was 17 years old. My parents and I had an argument and I left the house, left school and took a bag of clothes and never lived in my parent's house again. I stayed with an associate from school for about 3 months, met a guy and became pregnant with my first daughter. At this time I called home and told my mother who became very angry and told me "You are on your own, figure it out." My Grandparents disowned me and refused to talk to me. To let you know what feeling disowned was like, when 3 of my grandparents died I was not told about it until after they had the funerals so I would not show up and see all the other family members. It was like I was something that was to be ashamed of. I was something that should not be spoken about or seen. I have always been stubborn and strong willed. When I called telling them that I was pregnant I was scared of what was going to happen and needed the "mother's talk" (you know the one where mom tells you that you made a big mistake being so young but that everything will be okay, call me when you need to talk type of conversation). I didn't plan to drop out of school at 17. Nor did I plan to leave my parents house because of teenage pregnancy. I definitely didn't plan on living with the baby's father in his parents' house all in the same year.

His parents spoke only a little English and lived totally different than how I was brought up. His family was very strict. The women had to wear dresses down to their ankles without make up, earrings and hair cuts. They went to church 4 days a week. His family did not like the fact that we were living together and having a baby because their church members would talk. So at the age of 18 I married him at the office of the justice of the peace. The witnesses were the clerks that worked there. His mother despised me, believe me, she constantly reminded me that I was not doing anything correct. I was a bad wife, a bad mother and a bad person in general. She would tell me that I am too stubborn and hard headed because I wouldn't do what she wanted me to do. (To all the stubborn and hard headed people like me out there, being this way is not all bad it can be a blessing if used in the correct way, I learned this later in life so there is hope for all!!). Nothing I did was good enough for her, this is a family that believes that the men are kings and the women should do everything (and when I say everything I mean everything!). I was so unhappy being there I convinced him to get us an apartment and we finally moved out. I was left home with a baby all day and had to have hot meals 3 times a day on the table. Dinner had to be freshly cooked and ready when he got home around 11 every night. He didn't believe in leftovers. This is not to say that cooking 3 meals a day is a bad thing. It isn't! The bad thing was spending the time cooking and then being told that it was not cooked the exact way that his mother would cook it. Then it being thrown out and you have to start all over again.

The house had to be perfectly clean (white glove clean). I had to have his tooth brush ready with toothpaste and be ready to give him a bath. (Yes, you read correctly. I was expected to give him a bath like a baby; a grown man that was 7 yrs older then me). I was not allowed to talk to anyone but his family because he was a very jealous person, which limited my interaction with other people. A year later I was pregnant again. I was just getting by with the first child and here comes the second. Now I am really alone with much more responsibility and he doesn't want me around him or his family, except for his mother! She would always tell me that she would take my kids from me because I didn't know what I was doing. Once she locked me out of the house with my oldest child inside and I had to sleep on the porch because I would not leave; lucky for me it was summer!

It was hard raising a child with no help from the father or his family; I truly felt alone and helpless in the situation but I did it because no one was going to take my kids from me. I dedicated myself to making sure my children had everything they needed. Both emotionally and physically as I didn't want the same thing to happen to them as it did with my mother and me. Basically trying to do what I thought my mother could have done better with me. I had to learn by trial and error about babies, what to do when they cry, and what to do when they're sick. It was not easy as I could barely take care of myself never mind someone else that solely depended on me. My husband wanted nothing to do with raising the children. I was not lacking financially because their father worked, but I was lacking in everything else. No emotional support, no encouragement from my husband or any adult.

I was abused in every verbal way shape and form; degraded, taken advantage of, and treated as a slave and a prisoner all by his family who were of the Christian faith. They were going to church 4 days a week, reading the Bible every night, and still treated me like I was nothing; a nobody that was not worthy of anything. I could not do anything right in their sight though I tried very hard to please them. This made me shy away from church and people who went to church. I would be at church with them when the pastor was preaching and I would hear the Word and get excited about it, but then got so hurt because that was not what I was seeing from the family that claimed they loved God. They behaved one way in church and around church members, and then acted totally different at home. I was abused verbally then physically… (I will be honest with you; the physical abuse was not the worse. The verbal abuse did more damage to an already dropped person). I told his mother about what was going on and all she did was put the blame on me!

There I was screaming on the inside that I am not doing anything to deserve the abuse but what could I do? Her son could do no wrong. I stopped saying anything to anyone about it and stayed in a mess because of low self esteem with the thought no one would want me anyway. I can't do anything right so I might as well stay even though I was so unhappy and torn down. I was convinced I was not good at anything and couldn't do anything right because it was repeated to me so many times. I actually started to believe it. The one thing I would not accept was that I was a bad mother. This was the one thing that no one could convince me of. Being a mom, was the one thing that made me happy! People can say, "Well you stayed in the mess and if you were a good mom you would have gotten yourself and your kids out." My thoughts are: Please don't judge me or anyone else that has been abused physically or mentally until you have walked in their shoes. You don't really know what a person is going through emotionally, physically and mentally unless you have been in that situation. It is not an easy situation to go through, simply because you can't understand the condition of a person's mind unless you have been there. The mind is totally broken down at this stage. I finally got up enough courage to leave because I could not deal with it anymore and I wanted more for my children. I got a divorce after being married for 5 yrs. The thing which helped me get through it was, I did not want my girls to grow up thinking abuse was normal. I wanted them to have more. I never imagined my life turning out that way, but it happened…

Now that you know that part of my life you must be thinking, okay you got your self out and now on to better things… yeah right! Remember in the beginning when I mentioned that being dropped can cripple you and stay with you if it is not dealt with? Well I did not deal with it. Remember I just came out of an abusive relationship and 4 years later where am I again? I find myself in another abusive relationship, but this one is worse than the previous one. I still had low self esteem, still tried to please people, still wanted to be accepted, I was still broken, and still wanting to be loved. I found myself with a violent possessive person. You know how that starts, a person is all nice in the beginning but then…….. the true nature of the person shows up! I found myself in a vicious cycle, being abused by the father of my youngest kids. This is someone who said, "I love you and I will do anything for you." This is the same person that beat me and burned my face with cigarettes in one moment and the next moment said, “I am sorry I didn’t mean to hurt you; I love you so much that it makes me do crazy things.”

I was not allowed to go out of the house except for twice a month when we went grocery shopping. I had to get everything I need during those two trips because going to the corner store was not an option. I was only allowed to wear large clothes as not to show my figure to anyone. I wore baggy pants and an oversized t-shirt. I was told to keep my eyes down when we were walking and that he better not catch me looking at another man. I learned quickly about walking with my head down when he made a huge scene in a store, screaming at a man who did nothing but say sorry for bumping into me. When we returned home the situation escalated into three days and three nights of him yelling at me and hitting me. He told me I was nothing and no one would want me. He said I was totally disrespectful to him because I looked at the face of another man. I was allowed to talk with his sister but that only lasted for a short time before he was accusing me of liking his sister’s husband. At one point his sister and her husband lived in the apartment right beneath us. But it did not change anything because they did not want to get involved. He got in a fight with his brother (another person he accused me of being with) and he ended up being arrested. When he got to court the judge said he needed to be mentally evaluated and the court ordered him to be observed for a month at the mental institution in Worchester, Massachusetts.

This was my one break time in the whole relationship. I know you’re asking yourself how come she didn’t leave. No, I was afraid to leave. I was afraid he would find me and kill us all. While in the institution they had him in a straight jacket. He promised me he would change his ways and that he was sorry for all the pain he caused us. That was a lie! When he got out he was worse than before. His family knew his personality but could not do anything to change him, or the way he treated me. I was back doing all the things that I could possible do to avoid a fight. I tried my best to please him so I could avoid what would happen if I upset him. It seemed the more that I tried to do things that were right or things that I thought would make him happy the angrier he became. He nailed all the windows of the apartment shut so that we could not escape. He thought I would let someone in or escape out the window when he went to work. The mini blinds were checked everyday before he left as well as when he got home in order to make sure no one was looking out the window or looking in. This was in the middle of the summer and we were not allowed to have fans in the windows because he felt people could look in or I could look out. It did not matter to that we would be trapped if there was a fire. His jealousy mattered more than our safety. The doors both the back and front had a piece of cardboard wedged in it from the outside. He checked it to see if it was moved when he got home. I was told that he loved me so much that if I left he would have to kill me as he could not see me with anyone else. His behavior convinced me that he would kill me. He told me if I told anyone what he was doing to me that he would kill me and the kids as well.

I was not allowed to bathe before he got home as he wanted to check to see if there was any evidence of me doing anything with anyone while being locked in the house. If you were on the outside looking in you would never have known anything was going on. On the inside I was loosing myself and who God created me to be. Dying slowly and so scared for myself and my kids as to what he would do if I did something wrong or if I left. It was like living with a time bomb that could detonate at the slightest infraction like a small amount of dirt on the floor. He didn't abuse the kids physically but his abuse of me affected them to the fullest. He told me no one wanted me and that reinforced the low self esteem laying dormant in me from the previous relationship. I began to believe it was true. I was totally broken. Dropped again! The beatings and the threats were now hourly and not daily. He would not allow me to eat and I became very weak physically.

One day there was a knock at the door, it was the Jehovah witnesses and he did something that he never did before. He allowed them into the house. That was the biggest mistake he ever made! Two women came in and they sat in the living room for an hour talking about how much God loves His people. They gave me pamphlets on God. They asked if they could come back to do studies with me once a week on Thursday. God only knows why he agreed to this, but it was the best thing in the world to me. I was so glad for the company. They came every week for 7 weeks and I did my studies faithfully. I asked them ten million questions and even made them study themselves for the answers to give me. One of the women asked me on the 7th week how I was doing and I lost it and started crying. I didn't say much I just cried and I said that I was tired. I will never forget what she told me; she said that God loves me and wants better for me. She said, "Believe that God can help you when no one else can." When she said it I cried harder because I wanted out so badly but had no way of doing anything about being trapped in the house. She hugged me and told me not to get mad with her but she had to do what God instructed her to do. She asked what time he worked and if he came home during the day. I told her he came home around 7pm…that was the last time I saw her.

I thank God for her! She called a women's shelter and had one of the female counselors come to the house to talk to me about leaving. I told her I wanted to leave but I was too afraid that he would find me and kill me, and my daughters. She told me that if I really wanted to leave she would be willing to get me out. She told me that there are risks involved but it was possible. She left me her number and told me to call when I was ready. I tried to fix that cardboard just like he left it but it didn't work! I spent the next two days being beaten, tortured, raped, and my life threatened by a gun. Then he committed the ultimate trespass. I was bathing my youngest who was just a tiny baby and he hit me because he said the shades in the living room were moved and that must mean I was cheating on him. He told me I was going to pay and grabbed her in her little bath tub and held her under the water until she began turning blue. He kicked me to the floor and dared me to go near her. I defied him and got her anyway (got the beating of my life but she was okay!). I was not allowed to bring her to the hospital as they would ask too many questions and he would have to explain what happened.

That is when I made up in my mind that I was leaving. I could not allow that to happen to my daughter; he tried to kill her! I called the next day and they planned to come in three days and have a policeman at my house while they moved all my furniture. They told me they were going to move me and my daughters to a women's shelter in another state. I have never been more afraid in my life. When he came home I told him that we were all moving to a better apartment so I had to pack up everything. He believed me! I packed up everything and the morning of the actual move I was nervous, scared and sick to my stomach but smiled as he said that he would be home late. They came just like they had promised. They loaded everything in a truck and took it to storage. A policeman was posted at the front door for security just in case he decided to come home early! When everything was packed I got my daughters in the car and we were off to where ever they planned to take us. It had to remain a secret even to me until we left for the safety of the women who were already in the shelter. It was the longest scariest ride I ever had.... But I thank God for it. All the time from when I first told the women who helped me that I wanted to leave I kept thinking. Thinking what was I going to do now: how was I going to make it by myself with my daughters. Will I be strong enough to get out there on my own? What is going to happen now? Not knowing was the biggest thing, because everything had changed. I was free from him and didn't know what to do. It was good but very scary for me since I didn't know how to think for myself or make decisions on my own. I was used to living one way and didn't know how to live any other way. I stayed in hiding from him for two and a half years with the help of the counselors in the battered women's shelter network.

I received counseling for myself and my daughters, even though they were young, they also received counseling. I learned about self-worth and started rebuilding everything that was torn down. I had to learn how to forgive myself most of all. I blamed myself for letting the kids see what happened to me. I was ashamed of what happened. I had to learn that what I did didn't matter and the one that had the problem was him and not me. I learned to see myself as an okay person. I went from being broken to being made whole and I felt like I was starting life all over again (like a baby learning to walk but being an adult) it is harder because you are not just learning but you have to re-learn and reprogram what was told to you. I didn't want to forgive myself for what had happened because it happened twice! I wanted to punish myself for putting the kids through a mess yet again. I didn't think I deserved to be happy and I didn't know how to trust or to love myself. I learned with counseling and hearing others who have gone through similar situations that I was really a strong person because I was able to leave. I was alive and grateful, but it was a complicated process to learn to like myself and to forgive myself. I was able to smile again. I was able to live with out the daily fear of, what will he do next! I got my daughters out; I couldn't let them live like that and that was a step forward.

When I was finishing the special women's program I met my husband Bobbie. I was still working on myself as I had not fully forgiven myself for everything that had happened in the past. We started talking and spending more and more time together. He was different in that he wasn't abusive verbally or physically but what a mess he was getting himself into when he started dating me. He knew the word and would talk about it sometimes; not a lot at the beginning but mentioning it here and there. His positive way of thinking is what attracted me the most. I was moving to a new place in the same town and he wanted to go with me. We have been together ever since. The move and meeting Bobbie represented my biggest turn around (not to say that everything became "perfect") and helped me deal with my problems.

Bobbie's mother Winifred Edwards (Winifred Batts now) is a true servant of God. I never met anyone like her; she has great spiritual discernment. I had just moved into this 1st floor gorgeous large apartment and did not know the whole house was run by demons. One night I spoke with Winifred, who I call mom. My husband Bobbie (boyfriend at the time) fell out in the middle of the floor for no apparent reason. I was so scared and didn't know what to do so I called her to let her know. She told me about the house and how it was run by demons. She explained that if I wanted to live there, we would have to learn who God is and pray like we never did before.

I found out later that the previous tenant was a physic. This lady had the whole apartment painted black and had dolls hanging all around the ceiling and stars and candles everywhere. The cable man told me that he didn't want to come to the apartment because of what he had seen when the physic lived there. He proceeded to tell me that the bedroom (which was where my 3 youngest girls were sleeping in) actually had burned up because of someone trying to set the place on fire. There was demonic activity in the house and there is no other way to describe it.

The presence of evil could be felt all over the house. The windows moved like they were breathing. There I was with Bobbie, all the girls living in an evil house. I had no way of moving because of a lack of finances. So what was I to do? I PRAYED LIKE NEVER BEFORE! I learned who God was! Mom began that night to tell me about God. Now I need you to understand that I have been in Church 3 nights a week and Sunday when I was married to my first husband, so I knew "about" God. What mom did was explain who God was on a personal level. We stayed on the phone that night for about 7 hours talking about God as a real person. She told me what God did in her life. I have never met a more humble and patient person. She never judged me. She offered guidance and a better understanding of what to do and why I needed to pray and fast. Mom stayed on the phone with me everyday after that, hours at a time going over scriptures; praying for me and my family, teaching me, answering my many questions. Believe me, I had many of them and she had to ask God how to answer them all. She never took credit for anything. She always said it was the Holy Spirit that gave her the answers.

Once I started to look at God as a person with feelings, and love; my life was totally transformed. She told me that I was not crazy and God loved me! Me? Can you believe it! God loved this imperfect person who was dropped so many times and never truly knew it! With everything that has happened to me and the things I have gone through God loves me anyways! I developed a desire to read and study the word of God. Now I can say God truly blessed me! It was a wild experience because as I read the words, the words became alive to me! It wasn't just the reading but it was the understanding that I got out of the scriptures. It was being able to see what I was reading become like a movie right before my eyes. I could not wait until Mom got home from her job everyday to let her know what I learned that day. Some things she already knew about and some we learned together. The best part of the learning was seeing her get just as excited as I did. Sometimes Mom didn't get any sleep at night because we spent so much time going over scriptures or what I had read that day. She took her time with the guidance of the Holy Spirit and explained what I didn't understand. I can remember her saying, "now let me know if you don't understand anything that was said; I will go over it again and again until you get the understanding." She told me, "that God thought I was very special and unique! I was created by Him and I was not a mistake."

She was very patient me (with God's grace) as there was still things of the past holding me back from moving forward in God's path. I learned to look past the things that I have seen done in churches before. I began to understand that all people that say they believe in God don't really believe in Him. They say they love Him only with their mouth. Versus others that are really sincere and hold what God says as true and actually live by God's Word. I let what happened in the past with the church go... I started over.

Mom took us to church every Sunday. She knew that I was not perfect; she knew that I had issues. She liked me anyway! I found someone that no matter who told her what about me she still saw the potential in me. Just the way God does with His children. I really began to love God and was so grateful that He sent her to me. She became my mom and that meant mom whether I was with her son or not. She loved me like a daughter and she became my daughter's grandmother. I never had people close to me that really cared about how I felt or that truly wanted the best for me. What a change, what a turn around, what a blessing from God! These same things are what I wanted so much before in my life that I didn't have. Yes, I went through all that, but look what I have now, a whole family that will be there for me unconditionally and you can't ask for anything better than that! They are my family.

I am not sharing all this because I am looking for sympathy or because I want someone to say "wow she really went through a lot" I'm sharing this so that someone out there will know that they are not alone. When you're feeling small and helpless there is actually someone out there that loves you no matter what is going on. God is that person who is waiting for you to call on Him so that He can make changes in your life.

I find that along with the devil beating at my door, my biggest enemy was myself. Forgiveness is the key. God had forgiven me, but I still was not forgiving myself completely for all that happened. There was still guilt of my daughters having to live through that. Prayer and asking God to show me the areas I need to work on is the key. When He has shown me those areas, sometimes it is not the easiest thing to see, it is hard to see yourself. No one likes to see the negatives. It is much easier to throw the blame on the devil or on someone else. It is hard to be shown where I did something wrong or how I have to change some of my ways. Learning how to let go and let God, with the way that I think or how I see issues. Change, no one like's change (I know I don't) but I also know that change is necessary in order to get to where God wants you to be. Even though all these things happened I learned to keep moving forward (this is where the stubborn part of me comes in, refusing to give up). I have learned that God will always be there for me I just have to listen to Him and hear what He is saying. He has brought me a mighty long way from where I once was to where I am today.

I know that no matter what has happened in your life or how many times you were dropped, God will be the one to pick you up and get you going the correct way. It may not happen overnight but I guarantee if you give God a chance He will be able to change whatever situation that needs changing in your life. Don't give up! Keep looking up and keep smiling even in your storm. If you have breath in your body there is hope! Because there is a living God!

I want to encourage the ones that feel all is lost, that think there is no way out, that think they deserve what is happening or the ones that feel like it is their fault and they are ashamed like I was. Like it was told to me God wants better for you! The same goes for you, God wants better for you! God is not a respecter of persons. What He has done for me He can do for you. God helped me, He will also help you. What you are feeling; the shame, the hurt, the loneliness, the feeling of no self worth is not what you were designed to feel. There is another way, and there is someone that cares. (Really cares about what you go through) even if you don't tell anyone or you think that no one knows. He still knows! He wants to help. He wants you to feel joy; He wants you to be free! Free to choose, free to love and free to be loved. Just because someone is used to being abused, that doesn't mean that is how life is. Really, there is so much more out there! So much more happiness! The only reason I have overcome the "drops" and the birthing of Ishmael's in my life is because of the Grace of God and the people He placed in my life. This is the only reason that I am here today. I truly believe God was with me every step of the way. Watching, listening and waiting for me to hear Him calling me. I believe He saved my life and my daughters many times before I really knew Him.

A Son's Journey

Something simple can have incredible effect that can last a lifetime and then some. I think about who dropped me and wonder. Did they mean to do it? Did they see what they were doing and not care. Did they do it ignorantly moving according to knowledge that was handed down to them (or the lack thereof)? I find it hard to believe that my dad could have done something like that deliberately. However, I can't deny that it had an effect on me. An effect that lasted until I was a grown man, married and saved by God's grace through King Jesus.

He was never really known to me. I knew few things about him. He sang. He was in the Army (I thought he got kicked out until I found out he served 2 years and was discharged honorably...made me so proud of him). He loved laughing and entertaining people. His reputation was important to him. People showed him respect and valued his friendship. There was s side of him though that I never really knew. I have no real fond memories. Fishing was more a "him" thing than it was an "us" thing; him and me, but not us. No sitting and talking about anything of true value that I would carry with me the rest of my life. One piece of advice that he gave me (I believe it was the only piece of advice he actually took the time to make sure I got) had to do with having sex. I have to keep it real here because some fathers out there will do this to their sons and think they left a gem of wisdom when all they left was a rock of nothingness.

When you have sex with a girl, make sure there is no hair in the way or it can scrape and cut you from the rubbing back and forth. There it is. I was about 15 when he gave that advice to me. I had gotten hurt and didn't know how. My dad came in, checked me and handed me that gem of wisdom. Never left me either. Good advice, just not a good time. I was a kid. That told me it was okay to have sex with a girl who wasn't my wife, just don't get any hair in the way. Years later I still remember that day, not the date, but the content of those few minutes. He actually connected with me on something. You see, I never felt I lived up to what he wanted me to be or that he actually even liked me though I know that he loved me because he was my dad. Not sure that makes sense but somebody reading this understands me and that is why God allowed it to be written here.

He looked at me with disgust in his face. His words cut me but I didn't know I was bleeding till many years later. I was about 12 maybe 13 and had gotten in trouble with a school buddy of mine. We got busted for doing something pretty bad but pretty stupid too and my friend took the blame for the whole thing. I had to go to a hearing in the judge's chambers in order for him to officially confess and me to be witness to his confession and confirm that's what happened. My friend and I were laughing in the hallway later and I thanked him for taking the rap. He just laughed about it and was like, "Don't worry about it." I got home afterwards and my dad was reading a newspaper in the kitchen and I went to say hello. He said that a call came in for me telling me that all the charges had been dropped against me and that my friend was getting sentenced to a short probation for taking the rap. He looked at me with a look I still can't forget and, with a huff, ruffled the newspaper and said, "You're supposed to be a friend? What kind of friend goes to court against another?" I had just laughed about the whole thing with the friend who took the rap only to come home and feel like I was worthless, weak and disgusting in my father's eyes because I had broken some sort of law of honor that was yet to be known to me. He didn't like me.

Later, I spent years trying to be just like him in order to get him to like me and be proud of me. He showed me three things. A man drinks. A man has many women wanting him and available to him (including other men's women). A man has influence everywhere he goes. I excelled at these three things even as a kid after that day. I was an alcoholic by the time I was 13. I was extremely promiscuous. I was respected and treated as my father's son (a "young" man of honor) by men three and four times my age. My father killed himself when I was 16. I used to say, he even died like a "man"...he hung himself and hung on that tree THREE days. He couldn't do just one. Funny thing was that he did it on April Fool's Day. Go figure. It left me with an empty space to fill. Seek a father that would like me and be proud of me. I relished the stories of mobsters and found that I had a few in my family. I immediately was drawn to them and to the lifestyle of a "man of honor" as they called themselves. I acted like them, dressed like them, wanted to be them. All of this was in an effort to redeem myself in my father's eyes. I was not disgusting and a traitor. I was a man of honor. I was respected. I had women wanting me and I wanted them. I drank with the best of them and hung in there too. All three tenets of manhood, I lived. Do you like me, dad?

The disconnect I had with him carried into my life and affected me with my children. I was there but was disconnected. I was tough with discipline but weak in relationship. I didn't have a real respect for women. I treated them well but it was with a hidden (or not so hidden) agenda...control; influence. Suicide was always an option in my mind and really came to the forefront when I saw that I couldn't meet my young wife's demands of me as a man (husband, provider, and father). I felt the same thing in that kitchen when he looked at me with disgust when she got on me about how I was failing as a husband, provider and father. The answer...get mad, scream, break things, scare everybody and then seek to kill yourself as dramatically as you can. My kid's were scared of me. My wife was scared of me. Do you like me now, dad?

Coming to Christ was even an experience because I could not relate to God as a father but as a friend. A father doesn't like you if you mess up, but a friend always has your back. A father was not what I wanted God to be. My thoughts...Just be my "boy" (slang for friend), watch my back and honor our friendship. I promise to do the same. Years later I got to know God as my Father. I saw what a real father was like and was relieved that what my daddy was, God wasn't. How my daddy felt, God didn't and what my daddy did, God wouldn't. Now...neither would I. I could be like God and not like my dad. He dropped me. It affected me. This is just a bit though. There was so much more that it did. But that is a testimony that would take time to share.

I wonder though...did somebody drop my dad? Did somebody else drop that somebody? Hurt people hurt people and dropped people drop people. You probably remember reading that here. I lived it. I look back and feel bad for him. He missed out on so many things. He missed my changes, my babies, my marriage, my getting saved, my first sermon…So much. I wish I had gotten to know him and wish I could tell him that I forgive him for dropping me. I wish we could dig into his past together and figure out who dropped him so there could be healing for him. I can't though. He's gone. God's here though. He's an awesome Daddy. When I mess up, I still tend to ask, “Do you like me now, Dad?"

He always answers, "Yes."

BIBLIOGRAPHY

Conner, Kevin J. Interpreting the Symbols and Types. City Christian Publishing, 1992

Cunningham, Gene. The basics: A Categorical Bible Study. Bigelow, AR: American Inland Mission, Inc. 1990

Greene, Samuel N. Manual on Biblical Numerics: Published by Narrow Way Ministries

Leifer, Gloria. Introduction to Maternity & Pediatric Nursing. Saunders, 2003

Orr, James, M.A., D.D. General Editor. "Definition for 'PRIMOGENITURE'". "International Standard Bible Encyclopedia". Bible-history.com - ISBE; 1915. New International Version: Copyright © 1973, 1978, 1984 by International Bible Society

Random House Webster's College Dictionary: Copyright 2000 by Random House, Inc

Vallowe, Ed. F. Biblical Mathematics: Keys to Scripture Numerics. Forest Park: ED. F. Vallowe Evangelistic Association,
1995

Wycliffe Bible Commentary, Electronic Database. Copyright (c) 1962 by Moody Press)

CPSIA information can be obtained at www.ICGtesting.com
Printed in the USA
LVOW06s1735200915

454947LV00001B/38/P